ROMAN WICCA

PRACTICING WITCHCRAFT WITH ANCIENT ROMAN TRADITIONS & MYTHOLOGY

THOMAS PETERS

First Edition

Copyright © 2025 by Thomas Peters

Paperback ISBN: 979-8-9992428-5-3
EBook ISBN: 979-8-9992428-4-6

To my parents, John and Amanda, for teaching me how to be curious and open-minded.

TABLE OF CONTENTS

Section V: Recipes

INTRODUCTION

There is something spectacular about Ancient Rome. It was an empire that defied all odds, conquering the classical world and leaving a legacy that still shapes Western culture to this day. Its influence touches our art, law, language, politics, philosophy, literature, and even spiritual traditions. In this way, Rome has truly stood the test of time.

Today, with so much information available online, it has never been easier to learn about this magnificent empire. Interest in Roman history has grown to such an extent that it has even sparked a modern spiritual revival, known as *Religio Romana*. This neopagan tradition seeks to reconstruct ancient Roman polytheism through archaeology, literature, and devotional practice. Followers build shrines, leave offerings, perform daily rites, and even practice magic, just as the Romans once did.

These kinds of neopagan revivals aren't unique to Rome. Neo-Druidry has emerged from Celtic tradition, while Norse paganism has found new life in Ásatrú and Heathenry. Around the world, people are rediscovering ancient traditions as authentic ways to connect with the divine. For those who have felt discouraged or cast out by institutional religion, it offers an alternative form of spirituality that feels personal, rather than prescribed. It is, in many ways, a spiritual renaissance.

Wicca has certainly played a huge part in this cultural shift. Gerald Gardner helped popularize the idea that ancient practices could be reimagined for modern use when he published *Witchcraft Today* in 1954. It was one of the first books to defend the legitimacy of witchcraft as religious tradition for the modern age. He took something that many thought belonged only to fantasy or folklore and brought it back into lived reality.

Since then, Wicca has evolved quite a bit. While traditional Gardnerian Wicca followed a formal initiatory structure, many modern practitioners have adopted a more relaxed and solitary approach. The Wiccan God and Goddess are archetypal enough to be interpreted through a wide range of pantheons, which has allowed people to personalize their spiritual practice. Some witches use festivals tied to their ancestral homeland, while others may replace core concepts entirely with beliefs drawn from different traditions. Gardner might not have approved of such changes, but spirituality is, by nature, exploratory. It asks us to find what works, even if that means bending the rules a bit.

This book is an attempt to do just that—to explore the idea of what Wicca might look like if we bend the rules a bit and incorporate aspects of ancient Roman paganism into it. We will discuss everything from Roman mythology to practical rites and rituals you can perform in your home. You'll learn how to perform a devotional, how to cast a sacred boundary, how to celebrate the Roman festivals, and so much more!

Roman Wicca, like traditional Wicca, is built around the divine polarity of the God and Goddess. These are broad archetypes, but in our case, we will encounter them through the Roman pantheon of gods. Each deity expresses a distinct facet of the divine, like fragments of a greater whole. By studying their myths, we gain incredible insight into both human nature and our ancestral connection to the divine. In later chapters, we'll explore how to build relationships with these deities, so that you can call upon their areas of expertise in your magical practice.

Though I may blend many aspects of Wicca and Roman paganism throughout this book, I do not claim authority over these communities. I'm simply one practitioner sharing my path. This book represents an adaptation of Wicca informed by Roman traditions and my own experience and research. If something here doesn't resonate with you, feel free to discard it. Take what serves you and leave what doesn't.

Let this be your invitation to experiment. It can be a deeply enriching experience to incorporate such ancient traditions into your practice. Even if you don't end up using any of this information practically, I believe you will still come away with a deeper appreciation for the ways in which Ancient Rome continues to shape our world today.

Journal Prompts

1.) What aspects of Ancient Rome most inspire your curiosity, and why do they resonate with you?

2.) Reflect on a time when you "bent the rules" of a tradition to make it feel personal. What did you learn about yourself?

3.) List three intentions you have for reading this book and describe how you will measure your growth along the way.

SECTION I:
ROMAN PAGANISM

"Not to know what happened before you
were born is to remain forever a child."

—Cicero, *Orator ad M. Brutum* 120

1

THE OLD WAYS

Roman paganism, as it was practiced by the ancient empire, was a vast spiritual system that evolved over more than a thousand years, shaping the religious, political, and cultural life of Ancient Rome. While often compared to the religion of Ancient Greece due to its similar pantheon and mythology, Roman paganism was distinct in both its structure and emphasis. It was highly practical, civic-minded, and deeply intertwined with the Roman identity. Religion was not only a personal matter, but a public duty. The success of the state was believed to depend directly on the proper veneration of the gods.

The Romans believed in a pantheon of gods and goddesses who governed all aspects of nature, society, and human endeavor. Many of these deities were adopted from earlier Italic traditions or borrowed from neighboring cultures. Later, as Rome came into contact with the Greeks, many Roman gods were associated with Greek counterparts, though their character and functions often remained uniquely Roman. Jupiter, the king of the gods, was associated with the sky and thunder, and became the chief deity of the Roman state. Juno, his consort, was the protector of women and marriage. Together they ruled the *Di Consentes*, a council of the twelve most important deities in the Roman pantheon.

Unlike the Greek gods, who were often depicted in myth as highly emotional and impulsive, the Roman gods were portrayed more as dignified and authoritative forces. Roman religion emphasized duty, discipline, and order. These values were reflected in their approach to worship, which was marked by ritual precision and formalism. Every prayer, sacrifice, or festival had to be conducted correctly, as any mistake was thought to offend the gods and risk divine punishment. The concept of *pax deorum*, meaning the peace of the gods, described the state of harmony between the divine and the human world. Maintaining this harmony was essential to Rome's continued prosperity.

Public religion was central to Roman life. The state employed a highly organized priesthood responsible for overseeing rituals, maintaining temples, and interpreting omens. Among the most important religious officials were the pontiffs, who regulated the religious calendar and supervised sacred law. The flamines served as priests of individual gods, and the augurs interpreted signs from nature to determine divine favor. Perhaps the most revered religious order was the Vestal Virgins, priestesses of the goddess Vesta who tended the sacred fire of Rome. Their chastity and devotion were believed to safeguard the city, and their position carried immense honor and responsibility.

Temples were prominent in Roman cities and served not only as places of worship but also as symbols of civic pride and divine protection. These structures housed the images of the gods and served as the focal point for festivals and ceremonies. Important events such as military victories, imperial successions, or natural disasters were all marked by religious rites. Roman generals would offer sacrifices of gratitude after a campaign, and emperors often commissioned new temples to celebrate their divine favor.

Roman religion also included a rich tradition of household worship. Each family maintained a shrine, called a *lararium*, which honored the *Lares* and *Penates*—protective spirits of the home. Daily offerings and prayers were made to them, and significant life events such as births, marriages, and harvests were marked with private rituals. Ancestor worship was also important, with deceased relatives honored during festivals such as *Parentalia*, which served as a time to remember and nourish the spirits of the dead.

As the Roman Republic transitioned into the Roman Empire, religion became increasingly tied to imperial authority. Emperors were often deified after death, and in some cases, worshiped during their lifetimes. The imperial cult became a powerful tool for unifying the diverse peoples of the empire under a common system of loyalty and reverence. Temples to emperors were built throughout the provinces, and local communities were encouraged to participate in their veneration. While this form of worship was often more political than spiritual, it reflected the belief that divine favor was the key to Rome's continued dominance.

Roman paganism was also highly inclusive. As the empire expanded, Rome absorbed and adapted the deities of conquered peoples. Egyptian, Persian, and Celtic gods were often welcomed into the Roman pantheon, leading to a rich and diverse religious landscape. Mystery cults such as those of Isis, Mithras, and Cybele gained popularity, especially among soldiers and lower classes seeking personal salvation, initiation, and connection with the divine. These cults often promised rewards in the afterlife and emphasized inner transformation over public ritual.

The decline of Roman paganism began gradually with the rise of Christianity. While initially one of many mystery religions tolerated within the empire, Christianity's rapid growth eventually attracted suspicion and persecution. Over time, however, it gained favor among Roman elites and emperors. In the fourth century, Emperor Constantine legalized Christianity and began to support it publicly. His successors took further steps to suppress paganism. Temples were closed or repurposed, sacrifices were outlawed, and traditional rites were condemned as superstition or heresy.

By the end of the fifth century, Roman paganism had largely disappeared as a public religion. Yet many of its festivals, customs, and deities continued to influence later European culture. Elements of Roman religious practice were absorbed into Roman Catholic traditions, including the use of incense, candles, altars, and priestly garments. The Roman calendar, filled with pagan festivals, was restructured but never entirely erased. In literature, art, and philosophy, the gods of Rome remained a powerful source of inspiration.

Journal Prompts

1.) How does the Roman emphasis on civic duty compare with your current view of spirituality's place in community life?

2.) Identify a modern public ritual (parade, holiday, protest) that echoes Roman values of order and harmony. What parallels do you see?

3.) Describe one practice you could adopt to cultivate "pax deorum" in your daily life.

2

ROMAN DEITIES

Now that we have some context on what Roman paganism looked like in the ancient world, let's explore the deities themselves in more detail. Roman mythology includes dozens of gods and goddesses, many of whom were central to daily life, public festivals, and private devotion. Some of these gods originated in early Italic traditions, while others were borrowed and reimagined from Etruscan, Greek, or even Eastern pantheons. Together, they formed a deeply interconnected spiritual worldview where every aspect of nature, society, and personal life had a divine counterpart.

At the center of Roman religion stood the *Di Consentes*, a council of twelve major gods, often seen as the Roman equivalent of the Greek Olympians. Of these, three formed the *Capitoline Triad*—Jupiter, Juno, and Minerva—whose temple on the Capitoline Hill was one of the most important religious centers in Rome. These three deities represented authority, protection, and wisdom, and can be thought of in terms of a divine trinity.

Many Wiccans choose a patron god and goddess to guide their spiritual work, and the Roman pantheon offers a diverse range of deities to connect with. Jupiter and Juno, as rulers of the pantheon, make an especially strong Lord and Lady pairing. As we explore each deity in more detail, pay attention to which ones pique your interest or call to you spiritually. Lean into those relationships as you build your practice and you will create something really special.

It's important to remember that in Wiccan belief, each of these deities lives within the broader divine archetypes of the God and Goddess. When you are working with Jupiter, you are working with the God. When you invoke Juno, you are invoking the Goddess. Thus, we venerate the God and Goddess on a broader level, but also call upon their specific incarnations to access their unique spiritual toolsets.

Jupiter

Jupiter is the king of the gods, the wielder of thunder, and the divine authority behind Roman law and governance. He rules the sky, maintains justice, and ensures the protection of the state. His name literally means "Sky Father" (from dyeu-pater), and his role mirrors that of Zeus in Greek mythology, though the Romans portrayed him with more solemnity and civic responsibility.

As a Wiccan practitioner, you might invoke Jupiter in rituals of protection, law, leadership, or spiritual authority. His sacred day is Thursday, and he is associated with oak trees, eagles, and lightning. In spellwork, Jupiter corresponds to expansion, prosperity, and honor.

Juno

Juno is Jupiter's consort and queen of the gods. She governs marriage, childbirth, and the protection of women. While Juno embodies traditionally female roles, she is not limited to domesticity, as she was considered to be the protector of the Roman people and state.

Worship of Juno was widespread, and she had many epithets: Juno Regina (queen), Juno Lucina (bringer of light in childbirth), and Juno Moneta (advisor and guardian of funds, from which we get the word "money"). In Wiccan terms, she embodies the divine feminine in her protective, nurturing, and wise aspects. She is often aligned with the full moon, making her especially appropriate for lunar rituals that emphasize power, intuition, and guardianship.

Minerva

Minerva, the daughter of Jupiter, is the Roman goddess of wisdom, strategy, arts, and crafts. Unlike the Greek Athena, with whom she is often conflated, Minerva retained a more peaceful and constructive image in Roman culture. She presides over learning, medicine, poetry, and artisanship.

Minerva is a powerful ally in rituals for mental clarity, creative inspiration, or skill development. Her presence manifests as focus, so she is typically invoked when studying, crafting tools, or solving complex problems. She was traditionally honored during the Quinquatria, a Roman festival in March.

Mars

Mars is the Roman god of war, but unlike the purely violent Ares of Greece, Mars was also associated with agriculture, vitality, and civic strength. In early Roman tradition, he was a fertility deity who ensured the land would prosper. Over time, as Rome became militarized, his warlike aspect became more dominant.

Still, Mars retained his honor and dignity. Roman soldiers revered him as a disciplined protector of Rome. You might call on Mars when you need courage, when facing conflict, or when beginning a new project that requires strength and momentum. His symbols include the spear, the wolf, and the color red.

Venus

Venus is the Roman goddess of love, beauty, sexuality, and fertility. She was also believed to be the ancestor of the Roman people, through her son Aeneas, hero of Virgil's *Aeneid*. Unlike the often frivolous portrayals of Aphrodite, Venus was held in high esteem and linked with both passion and political lineage.

In spellwork, Venus governs matters of attraction, romance, pleasure, and artistic expression. Her festivals, such as Veneralia in April, were popular among women and focused on purification and beauty. Venus is best called upon during new moon love rituals or on Fridays, when her power is greatest.

Mercury

Mercury is the swift-footed messenger of the gods, ruler of travel, trade, communication, and trickery. He is associated with commerce, eloquence, and cleverness. He also guides souls to the underworld, making him a psychopomp.

As a magical figure, Mercury is invaluable for rituals involving negotiation, writing, digital communication, business success, or spirit communication. His energy is fast, witty, and transformative. In Western esoteric tradition, he might be compared to the Magician tarot card.

Diana

Diana is the Roman goddess of the hunt, the wild, and the moon. She is one of the most enduringly popular Roman goddesses among modern witches, and for good reason. She represents independence, intuition, and the sacred feminine in her wildest form.

Though often equated with Artemis, Diana retained a strong Roman identity and was worshipped widely throughout Italy. She is a lunar goddess, particularly associated with the waxing moon and with young women. Many Wiccans already venerate Diana under her own name, invoking her for feminine rituals of empowerment.

Apollo

Apollo, one of the few gods who retained his Greek name, is the deity of music, poetry, prophecy, and healing. Though more commonly associated with the Greeks, the Romans adopted Apollo as a solar deity. He is often paired with Diana, his twin sister.

Apollo may be called upon in rituals of insight, clarity, and illumination. He brings the light of understanding and harmony. While Sol is the physical sun, Apollo represents the intellectual and artistic radiance that comes from it.

Faunus

Faunus is the horned god of the wild, fertility, and prophecy. He is often seen as a rustic counterpart to the Greek god Pan, and he embodies the raw, untamed energy of nature. With goat-like features, he is a spirit of the forest who delights in music, sensuality, and divination. Faunus was also believed to speak through dreams and spontaneous visions.

To many Wiccans, Faunus is an embodiment of the God in his primal, fertile form. Sacred groves, pipes, and horns are all associated with him, and he is best honored outdoors under the moon or stars. He draws many physical and symbolic parallels to the Horned God Cernunnos, who was worshipped by the ancient Celtic people. In many ways, this makes sense, as the Roman Empire did eventually absorb the Celtic people during their conquest of Gaul. As a result, some Wiccans consider Pan, Faunus, and Cernunnos to be the same deity, just reinterpreted through different cultural lenses.

Flora

Flora is the Roman goddess of flowers, spring, and the blossoming of life. She governs the beauty and fertility of the natural world as it awakens after winter. While not as prominent as other deities in the Roman state religion, Flora was deeply beloved in popular worship, especially during the Floralia—a joyful festival filled with flowers, dancing, and theatrical performance.

For Wiccans, Flora represents the renewing power of the earth and the sensual pleasures of life. She is ideal for rituals involving fertility, creativity, pleasure, and personal growth. Flora brings softness and color to the practice, reminding us that magic can also be gentle, fun, and joyful. Offer her fresh flowers, especially in spring, or create floral garlands for her shrine. She pairs well with Venus, but her energy is distinctly rooted in the natural world.

Cybele

Cybele is the Great Mother, a primal and ancient goddess of the earth, mountains, and wild animals. Originally worshipped in Anatolia, she was adopted into Roman religion as Magna Mater, the Great Mother of the Gods. Her rites were ecstatic, intense, and deeply transformative. Cybele was served by a unique priesthood known as the Galli, who were known for their unwavering devotion and gender-transcendent roles.

Cybele holds immense power in Wicca as a symbol of the raw, ancient feminine. She is the Goddess in her most primal, volcanic, and protective aspect. Call upon her when working with deep transformation, healing old wounds, or reclaiming your power. Her sacred animals are lions, and her symbols include the drum and the mountain. Offer her red wine, music, or a moment of wild abandon. Cybele is a reminder that the divine feminine is not only nurturing, but also fierce, unbreakable, and eternal.

Vesta

Vesta is the goddess of the hearth and sacred flame. Her presence was central to Roman domestic and civic life. In every Roman home, the hearth fire was considered sacred to Vesta, and the public fire in her temple was tended by the Vestal Virgins.

Vesta is commonly associated with peace, warmth, and spiritual nourishment. She can be called upon when blessing your home, cooking meals, or during silent meditation. Lighting a candle in her name during ritual is a simple but powerful way to invoke her.

Saturn

Saturn is the god of time, agriculture, and renewal. He is a complex figure who represents a range of concepts, from wealth and decay to limitation and liberation. His festival, Saturnalia, was one of the most beloved Roman celebrations. It was a chaotic, joyful, and sometimes mischievous event where social order was temporarily reversed.

Saturn is also thought to be a wise teacher. He encourages patience, structure, and reflection. In your Wiccan practice, you might call upon Saturn during rituals of release, ancestor work, or in the dark half of the year when introspection is necessary.

Sol

Sol is the Roman god of the sun, a radiant force of power, clarity, and divine order. While Apollo later came to embody the sun's intellectual and artistic light, Sol remained the embodiment of the sun's raw, celestial power. He was often depicted driving a chariot across the sky, bringing light to both gods and mortals.

In Wicca, Sol represents the God in his solar form: a radiant, life-giving, and noble father figure. He is a perfect deity for rituals of energy, confidence, vitality, and truth. Sol can be honored at sunrise or noon, and is especially present on the summer solstice. Light a candle in his name to bring clarity to a situation or draw strength during challenging times. If you choose to operate within a divine polarity, Sol and Luna are a fantastic pairing, especially if you use celestial themes in your practice.

Luna

Luna is the divine moon, a goddess of mystery, emotion, and sacred cycles. Her presence is feminine, nurturing, and profound. The Romans saw Luna as a powerful celestial being who governed time, tides, dreams, and the hidden currents of life. She was commonly represented riding a chariot across the night sky with a crescent crown glowing above.

In Wicca, Luna represents the Goddess in her lunar form, embodying intuition, receptivity, and the power of reflection. She is an ideal patron for dream work, divination, menstrual rituals, or rites that honor the phases of the moon. Many practitioners align their spellwork with Luna's phases. A general guideline is to use the waxing moon for growth, the full moon for power, and the waning moon for release. Luna pairs beautifully with Sol, forming a balance of light and dark that are physically manifest in our world through the sun and moon.

THESE ARE JUST a few of the many deities available to you within the Roman pantheon. Beyond deities, you may also encounter Roman spirits, demigods, household deities (like the Lares and Penates), and even the divine personifications of virtues. Yes, the Romans worshiped words and phrases as literal deities! We will cover all this in the next chapter, as each of these can be integrated into magical practice when relevant.

As we dive deeper into Roman mythology, you may start to feel overwhelmed by all the names and definitions. Don't worry too much about this. Start with a few deities that resonate with you most and go from there. Build a shrine, light a candle, and speak their names out loud. See how they respond through dreams, coincidences, and feelings. Believe that the gods are real and are waiting for you to remember them.

Journal Prompts

1.) Which deity speaks to you most strongly and what personal attributes or challenges does that connection reveal?

2.) Sketch or write about a space you could dedicate as a shrine to a chosen god or goddess. What does it look like? What items do you have on the shrine?

3.) Compare and contrast the Roman pantheon to the gods of another tradition you know. What insights emerge?

3

ROMAN SPIRITS

When we think of Roman religion, it's easy to imagine grand marble temples and imperial processions, but the heart of Roman spirituality was more commonly found in the everyday. It was in the home, in the land, in the breath of the wind, in the fire on the hearth, and in the footsteps of the ancestors. For the ancient Romans, the world was alive with unseen forces and divine spiritual beings. These spirits were not distant or abstract. They were personal, local, and immediate. They filled the space between the gods and humanity in a way that made sense.

The Romans honored many of these spiritual beings throughout their daily life. These included protective household deities, nature spirits, ancestors, personified virtues, and even the human soul. From the Lares and Penates, who guarded the home and food stores, to the Manes and Lemures, who embodied the dead both remembered and forgotten, Roman life was full of spiritual awareness in the mundane.

In this chapter we will explore the rich diversity of spirits and divine forces that shaped the lives of ancient Romans. These are the beings who lived alongside the people, who received daily offerings, and who served as guardians, guides, and companions. For the modern Wiccan, working with these spirits creates a more intimate, grounded, and reciprocal magical practice. They allow us to build relationships with the divine that feel personal and alive.

We will begin with the household spirits: the Lares, Penates, Genius, and Juno, who represent the foundation of Roman domestic magic. We will then descend into the underworld to meet the Manes and Lemures, spirits of the honored dead and the restless forgotten. After that, we'll step into nature to discover the Nymphs and Fauns, wild spirits that hide in the forest. Finally, we'll explore the deified virtues, known as the Fortuna, Spes, and Pax, which offer symbolic value to practitioners of magic. These spirits may not always speak in thunder or fire, but listen closely. They are here with you now, just waiting to be remembered.

The Lares and Penates

In ancient Roman homes, no deity was more ever-present than the Lares and Penates. These spirits were the guardians of household wellbeing, protectors of place, and givers of continuity across generations.

The Lares were originally linked to ancestors, spirits of the family dead who had chosen to stay and watch over the living. Over time, they evolved into more generalized protectors of specific locations: the home (Lares Familiares), crossroads (Lares Compitales), neighborhoods (Lares Viales), and even entire cities (Lares Praestites). In this way, the Lares became deeply connected to the protection and success of the Roman empire.

In nearly every Roman household, a lararium was set up near the kitchen or entrance, which acted as a table shrine to the Lares Familiares. These shrines typically held small statues or painted images, incense bowls, and a dish for food offerings. The family would greet and honor the Lares daily or during special rites with wine, bread, salt, or fruit. The head of the household would perform these offerings to ensure that their family was spiritually protected.

The Penates, by contrast, were gods of the pantry and domestic stability. They were honored in conjunction with the Lares, especially during meals and rites of thanksgiving. These deities ensured that the household's food supply remained full and safe. Their name, derived from *penus* (storehouse), reflects their role as keepers of nourishment and survival.

For Wiccans, interacting with the Lares and Penates is a simple way to incorporate Roman paganism into your daily life. You can set up a modern lararium in your kitchen or dining room, offer a portion of your meals, or light a candle to these spirits before cooking. In doing so, you recognize that you are a part of a larger spiritual ecosystem that is here to help you and accept that positive energy into your life.

The Genius and Juno

The Romans believed that each person was born with a personal divine force: a Genius (for men) or a Juno (for women). This force accompanied you from birth to death, acting as the divine embodiment of your life force, fate, and potential. In essence, it is your past, present, and future reflected through the lens of divinity.

Honoring your Genius or Juno was a key aspect of Roman spiritual life. These spirits were celebrated on birthdays, invoked during rites of passage, and acknowledged in ceremonies of renewal. To neglect them was believed to weaken your own vitality, while regular devotion strengthened your inner alignment and sense of purpose. In this way, honoring your Genius or Juno can be seen as a form of spiritual maintenance, akin to cleansing or recharging your energetic field.

For Wiccans, the Genius or Juno closely parallels the concept of the Higher Self—the deeper, intuitive aspect of your being that guides, empowers, and evolves through experience. Working with this force can be a powerful form of self-directed magic, especially in rituals centered around affirmation, shadow work, or personal transformation.

One simple way to honor your Genius or Juno is with a candlelit meditation at your altar to reflect on your spiritual growth. On your birthday, you can leave an offering at your altar (a coin, a flower, or a written intention) to reaffirm your alignment with your highest potential. Speak to this inner divinity as you would a trusted spirit guide. It is not separate from you. It is the sacred spark within you.

This idea also resonates with many spiritual traditions outside of Wicca. In occult Kabbalah, for example, there is a strong emphasis on the soul's journey toward union with its divine source through inner alchemy and conscious transformation. While Kabbalah originates in Jewish mysticism and is not inherently Wiccan, its magical framework can complement Roman Wicca by offering techniques for aligning with your Genius or Juno. Both traditions view the self not as a fixed identity, but as a continually evolving process of seeking wholeness.

The Manes

The Manes are the spirits of the dead, particularly the honored ancestors of your family line. While the Lares protect the household in life, the Manes are believed to dwell in the underworld, resting peacefully as long as they are remembered.

The Roman festival Parentalia, held in February, was dedicated to honoring these spirits. Families would visit tombs, leave offerings of garlands, wine, and salt cakes, and maintain the spiritual health of their familial line through remembrance and prayer.

The Manes remind us that death is not an end, but a transformation. In Wiccan practice, they align with ancestral magic, especially useful in rituals that require guidance or protection from your own lineage.

One of the best ways to honor the Manes is to set up an ancestor shrine during your celebration of Samhain. This time is thought to be when the veil between the spirit world and the material world is at its thinnest, allowing ancestor spirits to cross over and manifest in strange ways. On this shrine you may consider adding photos of ancestors, family heirlooms, or anything that reminds you of them. Take a few moments to sit near this shrine and meditate on how your ancestors have shaped the course of your life. You can offer a libation of wine or honey for them to enjoy when visiting you. While doing this, speak their names aloud to call them home and keep them spiritually present.

The Lemures

Not all spirits come in peace. The Lemures are the restless or malevolent souls of people who have died without burial, vengeance, or closure. While feared by the Romans, they were not considered evil in a demonic sense. Rather, they were pitied as restless spirits, made dangerous by societal neglect.

To appease these spirits, the Romans held the Lemuralia in May. This nighttime ritual involved the head of the household walking barefoot, tossing black beans over his shoulder while reciting a protective chant: "*Haec ego mitto; his redimo meque meosque fabis!*" ("With these beans, I redeem me and mine.") The ritual was meant to exorcise or release these spirits from the home, acting as a form of cleansing.

For Wiccans, the Lemures provide a framework for banishing, cleansing, and boundary-setting rituals. You can think of any negative energy within a given space as manifested in the Lemures. When you are casting a circle or cleansing your home, imagine sweeping away these dark spirits from your space. For even greater cleansing power, you could invoke this tradition during a waning moon ceremony, using black beans as an offering or banishing tool.

The Nymphs

The Nymphs are wild and radiant spirits of nature, hiding within the natural landscape. They are found in springs, rivers, trees, groves, caves, and even in the mist that clings to the early morning hills. The Romans adopted their understanding of nymphs from the Greeks, but localized them to the sacred spaces of Italy. Every natural feature could house a *Nympha*, and many rural shrines were built where their presence was especially strong. Some were connected to healing waters, others to fertility, and some to mystery or madness.

To the Romans, Nymphs were not a spiritual metaphor. They were real presences that could affect the material world in chaotic ways. They could be generous and nurturing or wild and dangerous when disrespected. In Roman poetry and myth, they dance in sacred groves with gods and mortals alike, especially under the watchful eye of Diana, goddess of the hunt and the wild.

For Wiccans, Nymphs represent the raw, untamed magic of the natural world. They are much like The Fae, as is understood by European folk tradition. Working with them requires a strong connection to the land. If you live near a spring, forest, or river, you may wish to leave a coin, flower, or a song in their honor. Approach them with reverence and patience.

A simple ritual for the Nymphs might involve bathing in natural spring water with herbs and petals, asking the Nymphs to refresh your spirit. Whisper your intentions into the water and feel their presence moving through you like a cool breeze on a hot day.

The Fauns

The Fauns are ancient woodland spirits of revelry, mischief, and wild instinct. Often portrayed as goat-legged men with horns, they are close cousins to the Greek satyrs, though the Roman Faunus predates them as an old Italic god of prophecy and the wild. Fauns dwell in forests, fields, and uncultivated places—anywhere that resists human control.

They are playful and erotic, but not always safe. Fauns embody liminality. They exist between civilization and nature, day and night, dream and waking. To the Romans, they were known to cause panic in the lonely woods, but also to bless shepherds and farmers with fertility and good fortune. Faunus himself was honored in the Lupercalia festival, a wild celebration of fertility and purging that involved ritual running and playful chaos.

In Wicca, Fauns can serve as guardians of ecstatic magic. They can help pull you out of a rut in your life and remind you to move, dance, laugh, and howl. Their presence is especially powerful in rites that involve movement, intoxication, or trance. They love the chaos of it all!

You might invoke the Fauns when you feel disconnected from your physicality or natural instincts. A ritual could be as simple as dancing barefoot in the moonlight, lighting a wild herbal incense blend, or playing music and letting your body move. Ask the Fauns to help release inhibition and bring you into right rhythm with the world around you.

The Deified Virtues

Among the most distinctive aspects of Roman spirituality was the deification of abstract concepts. These were phrases honored as living spiritual forces, often with temples, statues, and festivals of their own. The Romans saw divine order not only in gods and goddesses, but in the qualities of a harmonious society.

Fortuna was the power of fate and fortune, both good and bad. *Spes* embodied hope and expectation. *Pax* brought peace and order. *Virtus* represented valor and strength. *Concordia* was harmony among people. *Fides* was trust and loyalty. Even though these are just words on paper, they were treated as active, divine presences who could be petitioned and honored, much like any other deity.

For Wiccans, working with these deified virtues is much like working with sigils or runes. You can write these virtues onto objects during your rituals to imbue them with the power of each phrase. You can even invoke them as gods and pray to them for guidance.

To honor a virtue, you might create a simple altar with a symbol, candle, and prayer aligned to that force. For Fortuna, a gold coin and a wheel. For Spes, a white candle and a written hope. For Pax, a bowl of still water and a vow to resolve conflict. These spirits respond to intention and alignment more than any specific or elaborate ritual. As long as you are genuinely trying, they will hear you.

Journal Prompts

1.) Recall a place in nature that has always "felt alive" to you. How might Lares or Nymphs help explain that feeling?

2.) Write a letter to your Genius or Juno, acknowledging its presence and asking any questions you have about your past or future.

3.) When have you sensed unresolved energy, similar to the Lemures? Outline steps you might take to bring balance to the situation.

4

THE AFTERLIFE

The Roman view of the afterlife was never rigidly defined. Instead, it was a flexible and evolving set of ideas shaped by centuries of tradition, regional folklore, foreign influence, and personal belief. For most Romans, death was less about divine judgment and more about ancestor veneration and remembrance. Unlike the sharply divided heavens and hells of later religions, Romans treated the afterlife as an extension of life itself. It was something to be acknowledged, tended to, and kept in harmony with the world of the living.

What truly mattered to the Romans was that their ancestors were not forgotten. It was extremely important that the proper ceremonies were performed during a death rite to ensure peace for the departed. If they were buried respectfully, honored through ritual, and remembered by their descendants, then their spirit could live on in harmony with the family. These ancestral spirits, which we now know as the Manes, represent a state of blessed rest for the dead. But if a soul was denied proper burial or remembrance, it could become a Lemure—a restless, troubled, or dangerous spirit.

Roman religion saw death as a transformation rather than an end. There was a prevailing sense that the soul continued on, though where exactly it went was never spelled out with universal agreement. Some believed that the soul passed into the underworld. Others thought it simply lingered near the tomb or returned to the divine source. Still others adopted the ideas of foreign cults that promised spiritual rebirth, purification, or union with a higher realm. What bound all these beliefs together was the conviction that the dead mattered. They were still part of the world, and they still needed care.

Ritual practice was the primary means through which the Romans maintained this relationship. At funerals, offerings were made, names were spoken, and tombs were visited so that the departed would know they were still part of the family. Some festivals, such as Parentalia, were devoted entirely to honoring the ancestors. Families would travel to the tomb with flowers, bread, salt, and wine to perform rites of remembrance. The dead were treated not as lost souls, but as spiritual elders, still capable of watching over the family and offering their protection. This kind of ongoing relationship between the living and the dead created a sense of continuity that stretched across generations.

While the official Roman religion offered little doctrinal clarity about what happened after death, the influence of Greek mythology and philosophy introduced more elaborate concepts. The idea of an underworld was taken directly from Hellenic models, representing a spiritual realm with rivers, judges, and divisions of reward and punishment. The virtuous might find themselves in the Elysian Fields, while the wicked could be punished in Tartarus. Yet these concepts were more symbolic than literal for most Roman citizens. The focus remained on fulfilling one's duties in life and ensuring that the proper rites were observed at death.

The Roman underworld was imagined as a vast and shadowy realm beneath the surface of the earth. It was ruled by Pluto, also known as *Dis Pater*, and his consort Proserpina, who had been taken from the world above in a myth that mirrored the Greek story of Hades and Persephone.

Within this underworld were many varied regions. Tartarus was the name given to the deepest and most dreadful part. It was not just a place of punishment for the wicked, but a symbolic representation of spiritual consequence. Great villains, traitors, and oathbreakers were believed to suffer there, bound by serpents or tormented by illusions. These myths served less as moral instruction and more as reminders of a greater cosmic order.

More pleasant was the image of the Elysian Fields, a sunlit meadow where heroes and noble souls dwelled in peace. Though not widely emphasized in Roman public religion, this idea appealed to poets, philosophers, and members of mystery cults. It represented a place of reward and remembrance, where the soul could find rest or even begin anew.

Despite these fantastical images of the afterlife, the average Roman did not obsess over their final destination. What they really cared about was whether they would be properly remembered by their family and community. In their view, immortality was found not in paradise, but in the continuation of their name. Tomb inscriptions often reveal this sentiment, with phrases like "I was not, I was, I am not, I care not," or more tender hopes that the earth would lie lightly upon the bones. It was the memory and legacy that mattered, not the metaphysics.

By the later imperial period, many Romans began seeking deeper answers through initiation into foreign cults. The cult of Isis promised rebirth and protection. The cult of Mithras offered purification and ascension through sacred trials. The Eleusinian Mysteries hinted at the soul's reunion with the divine through ritual knowledge. These cults offered spiritual promises that the public religion did not. They brought a more personal sense of salvation, introducing the idea that death could be a doorway to a greater truth.

The Roman view of the afterlife, in all its variations, offers much to reflect on for the modern practitioner. It tells us that death is not something to be feared or denied, but something to be honored through ritual, story, and presence. The relationship with the dead continues and the ancestors continue to walk with us always. They are watching, waiting, and listening. They ask only to be remembered, and in return, they bless us with their strength and wisdom. The destination doesn't matter, as long as we honor the memory of those that are there.

In Roman Wicca, this relationship becomes a central part of the practice. Ancestor veneration is no longer limited to just Samhain. It can be woven into the daily rhythm of your magic. When you build an ancestor shrine or whisper a name during a ritual, you are calling that ancestor into your ritual space. The Manes, blessed dead who guard the family line, are always near. They do not demand perfection... they just hope to be included.

Even the more troubling spirits, the Lemures, have a place in this cycle. They remind us that grief must be acknowledged, that unresolved pain can linger, and that banishing rituals have a sacred purpose. The Romans knew that not every spirit was at peace, just as not every emotion can be neatly resolved. Their rites of purification, such as the Lemuralia, were about setting boundaries between the living and the dead, ensuring that the home remained a place of balance. These same principles can be applied in modern spirituality when clearing energy, blessing a home, or protecting one's space from harmful influences. Put simply, acknowledge your chaotic thoughts, but don't allow them to gain any power over you.

Like Roman paganism, Wicca also has no fixed doctrine of what happens after death. Some believe in reincarnation, while others believe in a spiritual realm called the Summerland. Some even believe that the soul merges back into the divine or becomes an ancestral guide. All of these ideas can find parallels in Roman belief. What unites both is an understanding that death is part of the cycle of life, that the veil between worlds can be crossed, and that through ritual, remembrance, and devotion, the living and the dead can coexist in harmony.

In this way, I believe the Roman afterlife is better defined as a relationship rather than any sort of physical location. It is built from memory, cemented through offering, and kept alive by presence. As long as a name is spoken, that soul endures. In this way, there is no true death, only transformation, memory, and magic.

Journal Prompts

1.) What role does ancestor memory play in your family or culture, and how does the Roman view shift your perspective?

2.) Describe a personal ritual you could create to honor the Manes each year outside of traditional holidays.

3.) Contemplate the statement "death is a relationship rather than a location." How might that outlook soothe fear or grief?

5

DIVINE RECIPROCITY

The Romans believed that the gods governed every part of life, from the rise of empires to the harvest of wheat, and it was the duty of the people to honor them in return. This relationship was not based on fear or unquestioned devotion, but on a mutual understanding of reciprocity. If you gave to the gods, they would give back to you. If you failed to uphold your part of the agreement, divine favor could be withdrawn.

This principle was so foundational to Roman spirituality that it had its own term: *do ut des*, meaning *"I give so that you may give."* It was not a transaction in the modern sense, but a respectful acknowledgment of mutual responsibility. The gods were seen as powerful, conscious beings who appreciated recognition and ritual care. They were not omniscient judges removed from the world, but living forces deeply enmeshed in its order. They wanted to be included, remembered, and properly thanked.

To the ancient Roman, neglecting the gods was not just foolish, but outright dangerous. If a city failed to honor its patron deity, if a household ignored the proper offerings, or if a ritual was performed incorrectly, the results could be catastrophic. Droughts, sickness, failed crops, or military defeat were all interpreted as signs that the relationship between people and divinity had broken down. Maintaining this relationship required constant care. Priests, citizens, and heads of households all had their own responsibilities to ensure that the gods remained satisfied.

This model of sacred reciprocity offers a powerful framework for modern Wiccans working with deities. It reminds us that magic is not about commanding the gods, but communing with them. It is not about instant results, but an earned relationship. If you want the aid of a particular deity, you must first build a connection. You must understand their values, their nature, and their sacred symbols. You must speak to them, honor them, and offer something of yourself in return.

When you work with a Roman god or goddess, think of it as entering a dialogue. You are not just calling on them to fulfill your will. You are inviting them into your life. That means making space for them physically, emotionally, and spiritually. It can begin with something as simple as learning their mythology or speaking their name aloud. Over time, this can grow into more structured devotion, such as building a shrine, making offerings, or dedicating ritual acts in their name. Like any relationship, it takes time and sincerity.

Offerings are one of the oldest and most effective ways to initiate and maintain this relationship. In ancient Rome, offerings ranged from incense and wine to statues, animals, and even entire festivals. Today, the practice can be adapted in more personal and ethical ways. A libation of wine poured at your altar, a few coins placed near a shrine, a flame lit in silence with intention—these are all valid expressions of respect. The key is sincerity. Offer something meaningful, and do it with reverence. Food, flowers, herbs, oil, song, poetry, and even acts of kindness done in the deity's name can all be considered offerings. You do not need to spend any money, you just need to show that you care.

You can also express devotion through regular prayer or meditation. Speak to the god as you would a trusted guide or ally. Tell them what you are grateful for. Share your concerns. Ask for insight or guidance. Over time, you may begin to sense responses in feelings, dreams, and synchronicities throughout your life. These subtle impressions are how many deities speak. You are not imagining them, you have just finally learned to listen.

In Wiccan practice, it is common to work with gods based on their domain or specialty. This can also be done in Roman Wicca as well. If you need protection or spiritual authority, call on Jupiter. If you seek clarity and wisdom, turn to Minerva. For healing and light, look to Apollo. If you are crafting spells of beauty, pleasure, or love, Venus will likely be your best guide. For inner strength, courage, and movement, Mars answers well. Vesta is ideal for home blessings and inner peace, while Mercury assists with communication and business.

As your practice matures, you may find that certain gods begin to feel familiar. These are the ones who respond most clearly to you. They may not be the ones you expected, or ones you read about most often, but they *are* present. When that bond begins to form, deepen it. Spend more time with them. Research their symbols. Offer them gifts. Dedicate rituals in their honor. The more effort you put into the relationship, the more spiritual power you will draw from it. This is the path of divine reciprocity.

Unlike the gods of monotheistic traditions, Roman deities are not jealous. You may work with multiple gods, so long as you treat each with respect. The Roman pantheon was large for a reason. Life is complex, and no single deity holds dominion over every part of it. Feel free to call on different gods for different needs, just as the Romans did, but never treat the gods as vending machines. They are not there to serve you.

It is also important to follow up consistently with your deities. If you ask a god for something and your request is fulfilled, do not forget to give thanks. Leave a second offering. Speak your gratitude aloud. Let them know you noticed and are still listening. A relationship without gratitude becomes hollow, and the gods can tell when they are being honored and when they are being used.

Through divine reciprocity, the practitioner can walk with the old gods in the modern world. You bring them into your practice not as distant idols, but as spiritual companions. Over time, they begin to walk with you more clearly, more powerfully, more often. Treat this as a sacred relationship. It is built on trust, presence, and mutual exchange. The more you give, the more you receive. The more you open, the more they reveal.

Journal Prompts

1.) Recall a recent moment when gratitude transformed an ordinary act. How could you formalize that feeling into an offering?

2.) Draft a short dialogue between you and a deity in which you negotiate mutual responsibilities. What terms feel fair?

3.) List an area of your life where you might be treating the divine like a vending machine. How can you replace transaction with relationship?

6

ROMAN FESTIVALS

One of the most beloved features of Wicca is the Wheel of the Year, a sacred calendar that aligns spiritual practice with the changing seasons. It roots the practitioner in the rhythms of nature, honoring the cycle of life, death, and rebirth. But if we are to practice Wicca within the context of Roman mythology, then it makes sense to look to the festivals of ancient Rome for our own seasonal structure. The Roman calendar was filled with sacred observances, many of which aligned with the agricultural cycle, the solar year, and the movements of the stars. Though originally civic and religious holidays, these festivals can be adapted to fit the Wheel of the Year in a way that is still grounded in tradition.

The Romans did not have a single unified religious calendar, but rather a collection of observances that evolved over many centuries. Some were local, while others were imperial. A few of these festivals came to be celebrated across the Roman world and held deep symbolic weight for many citizens of the empire. These are the ones that will serve as our guideposts throughout the year.

Let's now explore a selection of major Roman festivals that correspond to some natural themes already familiar to most Wiccans: purification, fertility, abundance, transformation, remembrance, and renewal. Each one offers a chance to align your spiritual practice with the sacred cycles that governed Roman life and the turning of the year itself.

Februa (February 13)

Februa, also known as Lupercalia, was a purification festival held in mid-February. The name comes from the Latin *februum*, meaning "purification." It was originally a time to cleanse the city, honor the dead, and prepare for spring. It later merged with the wild fertility rites of Lupercalia, where priests known as Luperci would strike participants with strips of goat hide to bless them with health and fertility.

For the Wiccan, Februa becomes a sacred time to cleanse the self and the home. It mirrors the themes of Imbolc, a season of inner purification and preparation for growth. Begin your observance of Februa with physical cleaning. Sweep your living space. Wash your sheets. Open your windows and let the cold wind move the energy. Burn purifying herbs like rosemary or bay leaf. Add salt and vinegar to your water when mopping the floor to give it extra cleansing power.

Next, turn inward and bathe yourself ritually. You might anoint your body with a blend of olive oil and lavender while praying to Juno for strength and clarity. If you prefer to work at your altar, you can light a white candle and sit before it, reflecting on any emotional baggage that you are carrying from the previous year. Let it burn away into the element of fire while speaking affirmations for the months ahead out loud.

Juno is traditionally honored at this time in her role as Juno Februata, the purifier and protector of vital force. She brings love and sacred alignment to the world. Offer her milk, rosewater, or bay leaves. Speak your intentions clearly. If you wish to invite love into your life, then this is the season to open that door.

Parentalia (February 13 - 21)

Parentalia was a solemn and sacred nine-day festival dedicated to the spirits of the dead, especially the Manes. It was not a time of mourning, but of connection. Romans visited the tombs of their family members, brought offerings of bread, wine, salt, and violets, and performed simple rites to ensure that their ancestors were at peace. During this time, public life slowed. No marriages were held and no public rituals occurred. The city itself became quieter, more reverent, and more aware of the thin space between worlds.

The final day of Parentalia, called Feralia, was particularly important. It was believed that on this day, the dead were closest to the living. Offerings had to be made properly or the spirits might grow restless. Women often performed these rites themselves, bringing food and wreaths to family tombs. The relationship between the living and the dead was not based on fear. It was based on respect, love, and reciprocity.

For Wiccans, Parentalia is your sacred festival of ancestor veneration. While Samhain is traditionally observed as the time when the veil is thinnest, Parentalia offers a second, equally powerful moment to honor the dead. In the cold, quiet stillness of February, when the land is still asleep and the world feels quieter, the ancestors can speak more clearly.

Create a space in your home to serve as an ancestor altar. It can be as simple as a shelf with a candle, a bowl of water, and a photograph or object that connects you to your lineage. Light the candle at dusk. Offer bread and wine. Pour water slowly into a bowl while speaking the names of those who came before you. Speak to them aloud. Tell them how your life has unfolded. Ask for their guidance. Leave violets, if you can find them, or another white or purple flower as a symbol of mourning and continuity.

Let this also be a time for silence, stillness, and memory. You should read old letters, hold heirlooms, and look at photographs. Cook a recipe passed down through your family line. These small acts are magical devotions to the Manes.

The Manes' only desire is to be remembered. They are the roots and soil from which your life has grown. They are present in your blood, your breath, and your bones. If you honor them during this time, they will bless you. If you remember them, they will walk beside you in every challenging moment of your life.

On Feralia, the final day of the festival, you may choose to write letters to your ancestors and burn them as a sacred message carried by the smoke. You may leave coins or flowers at a local cemetery. You may spend the night in quiet reflection, letting their presence surround you. Regardless of what you believe happens after death, you can use this festival as a time to cultivate a stronger relationship with your ancestors in a way that feels meaningful to you.

Matronalia (March 1)

Matronalia was a festival dedicated to Juno Lucina, the goddess of childbirth, light, and new beginnings. On this day, women received gifts, and husbands offered prayers for the health and happiness of their wives. It was a celebration of feminine power, fertility, and the return of life after winter.

This holiday fits perfectly with Ostara in the Wiccan calendar. You can use it as a time to honor the divine feminine in all her forms. Decorate your altar with spring flowers and burn incense to Juno Lucina or Venus. Perform a rite to bless your creativity and power.

This is also a time to plant seeds, both physically in the garden and metaphorically in your mind as symbols of things you wish to grow in the coming months. If you identify as male or nonbinary, take this time to prepare a gift for a woman in your life that matters to you. It could be your mother, wife, grandmother, daughter, or even just a friend. If you feel comfortable with it, you can use this festival as a safe space to explore the feminine aspects of your personality. Meditate on how these forces shape who you are, regardless of the gender or sexuality you identify with.

This festival is also a fantastic time to perform fertility rituals. If you have been planning a pregnancy, you can call upon Juno Lucina's domain of childbirth and new beginnings to bless your fertility. This could be a simple prayer to her before conception or right at the time of ejaculation. If you prefer traditional Wicca, this could be a good time to perform The Great Rite.

Megalesia (April 4 - 10)

The Megalesia was one of the most ecstatic and primal festivals in the Roman calendar. It honored Magna Mater, also known as Cybele, the Great Mother. Cybele was a foreign goddess, originally worshipped in Phrygia, who was brought into Rome at a time of great crisis. The Sibylline Oracles had foretold that only her power could protect the state. So her black stone, said to be her sacred symbol, was brought across the sea and installed in Rome. Rites dedicated in her honor were said to be intense, chaotic, and transformative.

The Megalesia was a time of music, drumming, ecstatic movement, and sacred theater. Participants wore bright robes and played cymbals and flutes. Her priests, known as the Galli, were gender-nonconforming and performed extreme acts of devotion, including ritual flagellation and dancing into trance. While these rituals may be a bit too intense for modern sensibilities, the core of the Megalesia still remains relevant. It is about embracing the wild within, shattering limitations, and calling upon the primal feminine to break through the walls of spiritual stagnation.

In Wicca, this is your festival of initiation and inner liberation. You can use this time to challenge yourself, shed an old identity, or release patterns that no longer serve you. Consider creating a sacred space where you can move freely, dance with abandon, or make noise without shame. You might craft a simple drum or rattle for this purpose. Cybele only responds to raw emotion. Offer her something personal and handmade, like a woven cord, a poem, or a piece of bark with a sigil carved on it. You may even feel called to create an altar in the woods or under the stars to invoke her presence.

Call upon Cybele when you feel trapped or overwhelmed. She will break you out of the shackles of your own mind and remind you who you really are. Let this festival be your yearly moment of spiritual release. In that chaos, there is freedom to be found.

Floralia (April 28 - May 3)

Floralia was a festival of life in full bloom. Dedicated to the goddess Flora, it celebrated flowers, fertility, joy, and sexuality. In contrast to the more sober state festivals of the Roman calendar, Floralia was loud, colorful, and playful. Theaters put on performances filled with jokes and nudity. Women adorned themselves with bright clothing and garlands. Prostitution, often marginalized in Roman society, was celebrated and even ritualized during this time. It was a festival where life's pleasures were not only accepted, but sacred.

Flora herself is a goddess of flowers, gardens, and blossoming beauty. She represents the full awakening of nature after winter's sleep. Her domain is not only physical fertility, but creative abundance, sensual delight, and pleasure without shame. She reminds us that joy is a form of power, and that laughter, beauty, and sex are not distractions from spirituality, but vital parts of it.

For Wiccans, Floralia takes the place of Beltane. This is your celebration of desire, union, and vibrant life force. Decorate your altar with blossoms, especially roses, marigolds, and wildflowers. Light pink and orange candles. Wear clothing that makes you feel attractive and alive. Engage in rituals of attraction, glamour, or creative manifestation. If you are partnered, you may want to share sacred intimacy under the open sky. If you are solitary, honor your own body with pleasure, adornment, and care. There is no guilt in sacred delight.

Offerings to Flora can include petals, honey, wine, or perfume. You may scatter flower seeds outdoors as a living act of worship. Write love spells, beauty charms, or words of affirmation in her name. Celebrate loudly and without shame. Let this be a time to express your true and authentic self.

Vestalia (June 7 - 15)

Vestalia was the most sacred household festival of the Roman year. It honored Vesta, the goddess of the hearth, whose eternal flame represented the life and spirit of Rome itself. During this time, the inner sanctum of her temple, normally closed to the public, was opened for women to enter and offer prayers and cakes in silence. Flour was baked into special offerings called *mola salsa*, and the Vestal Virgins, guardians of the flame, performed rites to protect the city and its people.

Vesta is a quiet goddess. She does not demand ecstatic worship or grand sacrifice. Her power is found in stillness, warmth, and presence. She is the living fire in your home, your body, and your spirit. She is the divine presence in every meal you cook with intention, every candle you light with care, and every moment you protect what you love. For Wiccans, Vestalia is a sacred time of centering, home-blessing, and reflection.

Use this period to cleanse and bless your home. You might sweep each room with spiritual intention, anoint doorways with rosemary olive oil, or bake bread while singing or praying to Vesta. Light a single candle each day of Vestalia and sit in silence for a few minutes, meditating on peace and safety. Speak aloud a prayer of gratitude for the roof above you, the food before you, and the warmth within you.

If you have an altar, you may set aside a space for Vesta's flame. This can be a simple candle kept lit during the festival (only if it is safe to do so). Offer her flour, bread, milk, or salt. Listen to Vesta and she will help you to find sacred quiet in a life of chaos.

Sol Invictus (June 24 and December 25)

Sol Invictus, the Unconquered Sun, became a central figure in later Roman religion, particularly during the imperial era. While this deity took on a more formal cult in the third century, the reverence of the sun itself was ancient. Sol represents constancy, light, truth, and sovereign energy. He rides across the sky each day, never failing, never falling. His feast day on December 25 marked the winter solstice in the Julian calendar; the rebirth of the sun in the darkest time. His summer counterpart, celebrated around June 24, marked his peak.

In Roman Wicca, these become the solar pillars of your year. They are your solstices. The winter date is a festival of rebirth and is commonly associated with Yule or Christmas. During this time, light and hope returns to the world after a long winter. Begin your rituals in darkness and then kindle the flame of Sol. Burn a single candle at dawn and welcome him back with praise and gratitude. Speak your intentions for the coming year into the light. You may spend the rest of the day celebrating as you normally would for Yule.

On the summer date, celebrate the height of solar power, as Sol has reached his zenith. This is a time for rituals of illumination, strength, success, and healing. Wiccans may find it easy to associate this festival with Litha or Midsummer, as they fall near the same time and celebrate the same concepts. You should spend this time outside if you can. Raise your arms to the sun and feel its energy filling you with life. Light golden or orange candles on your altar. Offer citrus, honey, or sunflowers in Sol's name. You may write a spell or prayer onto paper and let it charge in the sunlight, or use this time to charge water with solar energy.

Saturnalia (December 17 - 23)

Saturnalia was the most famous and beloved Roman holiday. It honored Saturn, the god of time, agriculture, and liberation. During Saturnalia, social roles were inverted, slaves were allowed to feast as free people, and rules were relaxed in favor of celebration. Gifts were exchanged, games were played, and joy was everywhere. The phrase *"Io Saturnalia!"* rang through the streets. Though it began as a rural festival for the sowing of crops, Saturnalia eventually evolved into a celebration of spiritual freedom and role reversal.

Saturn is a complex god. He is the old king, the reaper, and the teacher. He gives structure and then teaches you how to break free of it. He reminds us that time is sacred, and that rest and joy are part of the cosmic cycle. For Wiccans, Saturnalia can be thought of as the build up to the winter sabbat. It is your time of release, reflection, and celebration.

Use this festival to release the burdens of the year and reflect on what you have learned. Write down what you wish to let go of and burn it with intention. Then, give yourself permission to play. Cook a special feast for family and friends. Share gifts with others, no matter how small. Let your altar be filled with symbols of harvest and time, such as grains, clocks, dark candles, and evergreen leaves. Honor both endings and beginnings in your rites and rituals.

If you have a coven, you can celebrate with a party! Invite residents to wear colorful clothes (*pileus*), exchange gag gifts (*sigillaria*), and share duties serving food and drink to one another to mirror role reversal. You can even elect a King of Saturnalia, who gets to decree light-hearted commands to anyone in the group for the day.

Saturn teaches us that through structure we find freedom. Through endings we make space for new beginnings. Let the festival of Saturnalia serve as a reminder that even the hardest parts of the year deserve a moment of joy, and that all things, in time, are renewed.

As you can see, the Roman calendar offers a rich and vibrant alternative to the Wheel of the Year. Its festivals align with many of the same natural rhythms that Wiccans already celebrate—birth, growth, harvest, death, and rebirth—but through the lens of Roman spirituality and culture. By following this cycle, you are participating in a living tradition that honors the Roman gods as real forces shaping your life. You are telling the gods you remember them, and in return, they will remember you.

Journal Prompts

1.) Choose one festival that excites you. Plan a modern observance and note which symbols, foods or actions you will include.

2.) Reflect on the balance of solemnity and celebration in Roman holidays. Where do you tend to lean, and what might the opposite teach you?

3.) How might aligning with the Roman cycle enhance or detract your awareness of seasonal change in your own climate?

7

DAILY DEVOTIONALS

Daily devotionals are one of the most effective ways to deepen your relationship with the Roman gods. In ancient times, Romans honored the divine in small, consistent acts throughout their daily life. This was far more important than any grand festival. These quiet moments of reverence helped maintain the *pax deorum*, the peace between humans and the gods, and maintained spiritual harmony in the home.

In Wicca, daily devotionals can serve a similar purpose. They can create rhythm and consistency in your practice while deepening your relationship to your patron god or goddess. If, for instance, you are planning on performing a ritual to gain divine insight, you may want to perform daily devotionals to Minerva in the days prior, as she is the goddess of clarity. Once you have established a relationship, you can then call upon her expertise to empower your ritual. Rather than waiting for a sabbat, you are keeping the divine close through these frequent and intentional acts of connection.

Your devotional does not need to be long. Even five minutes a day of sincere attention is enough. What matters is consistency and intention. As a guideline, let's walk through how a devotional might be structured.

1.) Approach with purpose

Begin your devotional by mentally preparing yourself. This can be as simple as washing your hands, lighting incense, or taking a few deep breaths. Approach your altar or shrine as if you are entering a sacred space. Even if the space is humble, your intention transforms it. Speak aloud a clear statement of intent, for example:

> *"I stand before the gods in reverence and truth."*

2.) Light a candle

Light a candle in the center of your altar or shrine to represent the divine presence. This can be a flame for Vesta, for your chosen deity, or for the God and Goddess as a unified whole. You may also ring a bell to mark the start of the offering.

3.) Make an offering

Offer something physical to the divine. This can be a few drops of wine, a pinch of herbs, a flower, or even water. Place it in a small plate or bowl on your altar. As you offer it, say:

> *"To [Deity], I offer this gift.*
> *May it please you and keep our bond strong."*

If you are not working with a specific god yet, you can offer it generally:

> *"To the gods of Rome, known and unknown,*
> *I give this gift in honor and love."*

4.) Speak a prayer

Recite a short prayer to the deity you are honoring. You can write your own, repeat a traditional invocation, or simply speak from the heart. Here are a few examples:

"Jupiter, bringer of justice, grant me clarity and strength today."

"Venus, goddess of beauty, let love and kindness fill my words."

"Diana, guardian of the wild, help me walk my path with courage."

You do not need to sound poetic. Speak honestly. Over time, you may build a collection of personal prayers that become your own devotional liturgy.

5.) Meditate and reflect

Spend a few quiet moments in meditation or reflection. You may visualize the deity, hold a sacred object, or simply close your eyes and listen. This is not a time to ask for things. It is a time to be present. Make sure you are listening, not speaking.

6.) Close with gratitude

When you feel complete, thank your patron god aloud. For example:

"[Deity], I thank you for your presence.
May your wisdom remain with me."

Extinguish the flame or let it burn down naturally (if it is safe to do so). Ring the bell again if you began with one. Leave the offering on your shrine until the next day, then dispose of it respectfully in nature or your compost bin. It is not the item itself that matters, but the intention carried with it.

The God of the Day

As you get more comfortable performing devotionals, you may decide to honor multiple gods at once throughout the week. This is not about cutting corners, but rather establishing a wide net of relationships. Just as you may text several friends throughout the week, here you are building multiple friendships in parallel with different deities. Each day can be dedicated to a different Roman deity, based on their ancient planetary associations (see chapter 10 for more details).

Sunday: Sol
Monday: Luna
Tuesday: Mars
Wednesday: Mercury
Thursday: Jupiter
Friday: Venus
Saturday: Saturn

DON'T LET your devotionals become stagnant. They should change as you do. Some people may prefer to perform special devotionals during the Roman festivals. For example, during Floralia, you may include prayers for joy and creativity. During Parentalia, you may honor your ancestors more directly. You could even write or rotate your own prayers for different moods or intentions. A morning prayer might focus on guidance, while an evening one might focus on peace. You may even choose to pull an oracle or tarot card after your devotional as a way to receive guidance from the gods. All these small additions help your devotionals feel like an exciting part of your spiritual practice and ensures that your relationship with the gods evolves as you do.

What makes devotionals so powerful is not their complexity, but their constancy. You are showing up for the gods every day. Even when life feels mundane or rushed, you are creating a sacred rhythm that builds spiritual momentum.

Eventually, the gods *will* begin to respond. This may not always be in loud or miraculous ways, but in subtle nudges, vivid dreams, and moments of peace that arise for no reason. That is how you will know they are near. Through devotionals, you are drawing them even closer.

There is no set way to perform a devotional. Whether you have five minutes or fifty, one candle or a full altar, your sincerity is what the gods notice most. If devotionals begin to feel like a chore to you, then it's usually a sign to change up your formula. Write a new prayer or try offering song and dance as an offering. You can also try just sitting in silent contemplation instead of speaking anything. If you're bored, then you can *bet* the gods are too. A devotional should feel exciting, so find what works for you!

Journal Prompts

1.) Map a five-minute morning or evening devotional routine you can realistically keep for one month.

2.) Track how your mood and intuition shift over seven days of consistent devotion; journal observations daily.

3.) Consider a deity whose virtues you need right now. What small, repetitive act could honor that deity between larger rites?

SECTION II:
ROMAN MAGIC

In Ancient Rome, magic was woven into the fabric of daily life, neither fully separate from religion nor entirely under its control. It operated in the spaces between official rites and personal need, drawing on tradition, intuition, and unseen forces. In this section, we will explore aspects of Roman magic that can be adapted into your own magical practice.

8

RITUAL TOOLS

Ritual is the beating heart of any magical tradition. It is through sacred acts, gestures, and tools that unseen forces are made visible, and the spiritual becomes tangible. In Wicca, tools serve as bridges between the material world and the divine. They focus intention, direct energy, and act as vessels for sacred power. In Roman Wicca, our ritual tools are rooted in both the traditional instruments of Roman religion and the adapted practices of modern witchcraft. These tools are both symbolic and functional. They are sacred extensions of your will and your devotion to the path.

The ancient Romans used ritual tools with incredible precision. Every gesture, placement, and material had an intentional meaning. Public priests, such as the flamines and pontiffs, performed ceremonies that demanded absolute ritual correctness. Omitting a word or using the wrong implement could invalidate the entire rite, leading to disastrous consequences. While Wicca does not require that same degree of rigidity, it does inherit the reverence for sacred instruments. Each tool you include in your practice should be chosen with intention, cleansed before use, and treated with respect.

Below you will find an outline of the core tool kit of Roman Wicca. Each item has historical lineage, spiritual function, and magical application. You may choose to use all of them, or only those that resonate with your practice. These tools are the hands of your rituals. Through them, you can step fully into Roman tradition.

The Focus

The focus was a sacred hearth or fire used in both public and private Roman ritual. In Wicca, the focus becomes the central flame of your ritual space. It represents Vesta, the goddess of the hearth, as well as the divine spark within all acts of magic.

You may use a single candle on your altar as your focus, or construct a small fire in a fire-safe cauldron or brazier. Light it at the beginning of your ritual, and speak a prayer of invocation. Let the flame be your witness and your offering. At the end of the ritual, extinguish it slowly and with reverence, never blowing it out casually. If you have a fireplace in your home, you can use this as your focus when performing hearth or kitchen magic.

The focus can also be used for burning petitions, herbs, or incense. It is the center of power, where energies are offered and released. If your space allows, you can use it as a cauldron to burn loose leaf incense using a charcoal disc. Keep it clean, stable, and elevated. In every rite, treat the flame as divine presence. You are not just lighting a candle, but invoking the sacred element of fire.

The Simpulum

The *simpulum* was a small ladle used by Roman priests to pour libations during rituals. It is one of the most iconic tools of Roman religion, often seen in statues and carvings of the flamines. In Wicca, the simpulum can be used to offer liquid libations to the gods—usually wine, milk, water, oil, or honey. You can use it in ritual or to transfer offerings to your deity shrines.

Your simpulum does not have to be ornate. It can be a brass ladle, a handcrafted cup, or a small bowl with a pouring lip. What matters is that it is only used for ritual purposes. Before each use, cleanse it and bless it. When offering liquid to a deity, always speak aloud your intention. Pour slowly, either into the earth, into a libation bowl, or near a deity statue on your altar.

The Patera

The *patera* was a flat, shallow dish used in Roman ritual to present offerings such as wine, incense, fruit, or grain. Often made of bronze or ceramic, it was held with the thumb looped through the handle in a way that kept the offering stable during invocation. If you aren't concerned with historical accuracy, any nice plate or dish will work just fine as a patera.

In Wicca, the patera becomes the vessel through which you make your devotion visible. It may hold any physical offering, like cakes, nuts, herbs, coins, or salt. It can also be used to hold water for aspersion or ritual washing. The key is to use it with intention. Prepare your offering, place it carefully in the dish, and raise it toward your deity or altar flame. Speak aloud your dedication, even if it is only a few words. You can then leave the patera with your offering on the altar or shrine for as long as you want.

Choose a patera that feels right in your hands. It does not need to be antique or historically perfect recreation. What matters is that you hold reverence when you use it. It is a tool of presentation, so it should make your offerings look as enticing as possible. If you must use a bowl or plate from your kitchen, try to use the most ornate or beautiful one that you can find. It should feel extra special to you if possible.

The Aspergillum

The *aspergillum* was a ritual sprinkler used to cast holy water in purification rites. Roman priests would dip it into a vessel of blessed water and sprinkle participants or sacred spaces. This tool was believed to cleanse the body and the spirit, creating sacred space for divine presence.

In Wicca, the aspergillum can be used to cleanse the ritual area, your altar, and yourself before magical work. You can make your own by tying herbs, such as rosemary or hyssop, into a small bundle and dipping it into consecrated water. Shake it gently over the space while reciting a prayer of purification. You may also use a simple branch or handcrafted tool with a woven or bristled end.

Keep a small bowl of water nearby, perhaps with salt or a drop of wine added. This becomes your *aqua lustralis*, the sacred water. Use it sparingly but intentionally. As you sprinkle, visualize the removal of stale energy, distractions, or spiritual residue. You are preparing your space into a sacred temple of worship.

The Lituus

The *lituus* was a curved staff used by Roman augurs when interpreting omens from the sky. It symbolized the authority to divide the heavens and discern the will of the gods. Though originally a tool of divination, it also became a ceremonial emblem of spiritual authority.

In Wicca, the lituus may serve multiple roles. It can be used in formal ceremonies as a wand or staff, marking the sacred boundary of your circle. It may also be kept on your altar as a symbol of divinatory insight or augury. For those who practice Roman-style divination, whether through birds, dice, or celestial omens, the lituus becomes a practical tool you can use at any time to draw ritual boundaries and divine messages from the sky.

Your lituus may be a simple walking staff carved with symbols, or a ritual wand bent slightly at the end to mimic the ancient shape. When using it, touch the ground lightly as you walk, trace sacred circles in the air, or lift it in invocation. Use it as an extension of your will.

The Thurible

Incense was a central feature of Roman ritual. It carried prayers upward, sanctified the air, and pleased the gods through scent and smoke. The censer, or *thurible*, was used to burn incense grains like frankincense, myrrh, or storax. Roman priests carried them in processions, and they were placed on altars during almost every rite.

In Wicca, the censer is your tool of invocation and transformation. It marks the space as sacred and prepares the senses for ritual. It attracts divine presence and clears away spiritual stagnation. You can use charcoal disks in a fireproof bowl, a traditional hanging censer, or cauldron if you like. Burn resins, herbs, or ground offerings and let the smoke rise slowly. Watch it move and see if you can divine messages from the way the smoke swirls around you.

Each god has their own preferred scent. Jupiter favors frankincense. Venus prefers rose or cinnamon. Vesta responds to laurel and cedar. You should learn the correspondences and always make sure you offer the right scent. Light the censer at the beginning of your rituals and let the smoke carry your affirmations to the divine as you practice your magic.

The Bell

While not uniquely Roman, bells were used in temples and domestic shrines across the ancient world to ward off evil and announce the arrival of the sacred. Sound has always been a powerful force in ritual. It cuts through space and clears energy. It signals the beginning and end of spiritual work.

In Wicca, the bell is used to open and close ritual, to cleanse the air, or to call spirits into presence. It is the voice of your altar. Choose a bell with a clear, resonant tone. Strike it three times at the beginning of ritual to call the gods. Strike it once at the end to dismiss them with thanks. You may also use it during purification rites, ringing it while sprinkling water or wafting incense.

THESE TOOLS FORM the basic ritual set of Roman Wicca. Each has a purpose and carries a spiritual lineage that reaches back to the temples, shrines, and hearths of Ancient Rome. You do not need to acquire them all at once. Start with what speaks to you or craft what you can. Make sure to consecrate each tool with care, ideally with all four elements. Let your relationship with them grow over time as you use them in your practice.

Treat them with reverence, but don't be afraid to *really* use them in your rituals. They are not museum pieces. They are real instruments of magic and transformation. When you hold them, remind yourself that you are holding the weight of tradition and the presence of gods. They are active, right at your very fingertips.

Journal Prompts

1.) Inventory the tools you already own that could serve ritual purposes; note their mundane and sacred uses.

2.) Imagine crafting or repurposing one item by hand. What does it look like? What personal symbolism will it carry?

3.) Reflect on how the Roman attitude of precision influences your feelings about ritual preparation.

9

THE SACRED BOUNDARY

I n Roman Wicca, the sacred boundary will act as the spiritual container in which your rituals take place. It is a protected space that marks the separation between the mundane world and the sacred realm. In traditional Wicca, this is called "casting a circle," but the Roman version draws on older and more civic-based ideas of boundary, space, and sanctity. Rather than forming a mystical bubble of energy, you are establishing a sacred perimeter that echoes the Roman concepts of the *pomerium* and *templum*, spaces set aside for divine presence and human reverence.

The pomerium was the sacred boundary of the city of Rome, ritually plowed and set apart by augurs and priests. It acted as a spiritual threshold between the human world and the divine. No military action could be taken within it and no outsider could cross it without permission. It was inviolate, made holy through the authority of ritual.

A powerful way to honor this concept, and one that many Wiccans already do, is to mark your sacred boundary in the physical world with dirt, rocks, crystals, salt, or sand. For historical accuracy, you can step outside and draw the perimeter directly into the dirt with a staff or lituus. If marking a physical boundary is not possible, simply draw out the perimeter with your finger and imagine it surrounding you in your mind's eye.

The templum was another kind of sacred space. It referred not only to temples, but to any area that had been ritually consecrated and marked out for communication with the gods. Augurs would use a lituus to divide the heavens into sections, interpreting signs from birds or stars within that framework. The space was seen as oriented, measured, and aligned with the divine cosmos. Wiccans do this as well, aligning our sacred circles with the four cardinal points and cleansing our space with the four elements.

When you cast a sacred boundary for your rituals, you are essentially declaring your ritual space as a sacred temple. You are announcing to the gods and spirits that this area has been cleared, marked, and set aside for divine interaction. It is both a boundary and a vessel. It keeps harmful forces out, while keeping sacred presence in.

While a sacred boundary is not always necessary to perform magic, it does significantly help shift your awareness into a higher state of consciousness. It can be especially useful for more intense spiritual work, allowing your mind closer and safer access to the spirit world. With regards to historical accuracy, Roman priests *always* performed rituals within marked and purified spaces. This was something that was pretty much non-negotiable, as ritual accuracy was a top priority.

The sacred boundary has historically been used to show respect to the gods. When you set it intentionally, you are telling the gods that you have prepared a proper space for them to join you. You are creating a spiritual offering through structure and clarity. Just as you would clean and prepare your home for honored guests, you do the same for these divine beings.

1.) Prepare the space

Before you establish a sacred boundary, take time to physically and spiritually clean the space. Sweep the floor and clear out any clutter you see. Burn incense associated with cleansing or use an aspergillum to sprinkle sacred water around the space. Speak aloud your intentions and make it known that you are cleaning this space to prepare it for the gods themselves.

Next, place your ritual tools, offerings, and focus flame at the center of your working area. This becomes your *focus templum*, the heart of your ritual. Wiccans know it as the altar. You may use a candle, a bowl of water, or images of your patron deities to anchor this center. Make sure you have everything you need prepared in front of you. Once everything is in its place, you are ready to mark the boundary.

2.) Orient yourself east

Face east. This is the traditional direction of beginnings and sacred light. It is where Roman augurs began their observations and where many spiritual traditions, including Wicca, start their rites. Stand at the edge of your ritual space and hold your lituus or wand up.

3.) Speak an invocation of place

Speak aloud your purpose. Declare that you are setting this space apart for sacred work. For example, you may say:

"By sacred flame and ancient right,
fill this space with holy light.
Let none who walk with ill intent,
find themselves where gods are sent.
Within these bounds let virtue reign,
Let peace reside and truth remain."

4.) Trace the perimeter

Slowly walk the outer edge of your ritual space in a clockwise direction. As you walk, trace the boundary with your lituus or wand. You may imagine a white flame or golden line forming around you. As you walk, chant or speak:

> *"O flame of Vesta, ever bright,*
> *I cast this boundary in your light.*
> *By Rome's own hand and gods above,*
> *I seal this space with law and love."*

Complete the boundary and return to your starting point in the east.

5.) Call the Four Winds (optional)

While not traditionally Roman, Wiccans often invoke elemental guardians or directional forces into their sacred space. If you wish to include them, you may call them in as Roman personifications of the winds. To do this, we must mark the four cardinal points of our boundary with a candle, ideally a colored candle that corresponds to their domain.

Vulturnus is the Eastern spirit of the dawn and the spring winds. Auster is the Southern spirit of fire and summer storms. Favonius is the Western wind of flower and renewal, and Aquilo is the Northern wind of winter and clarity. Now, continuing on with our ritual, let's invoke these winds into our sacred space.

Walk to the Eastern cardinal point of your boundary. Light a yellow candle here as you say:

> *"Hail Vulturnus, guardian of the East, bringer of Air's clarity,*
> *I invoke your power and presence into this sacred space."*

Walk to the Southern cardinal point of your boundary. Light a red candle here as you say:

> *"Hail Auster, guardian of the South, bringer of Fire's strength,*
> *I invoke your power and presence into this sacred space."*

Walk to the Western cardinal point of your boundary. Light a blue candle here as you say:

"Hail Favonius, guardian of the West, bringer of Water's flow, I invoke your power and presence into this sacred space."

Walk to the Northern cardinal point of your boundary. Light a green candle here as you say:

"Hail Aquilo, guardian of the North, bringer of Earth's stability, I invoke your power and presence into this sacred space."

Now stand in the center of your sacred boundary and feel the presence of these four winds entering your space. It may feel like a warmth in your hands or a tingle on your body. Welcome them and thank them for their attendance.

6.) Light the central flame

Now that the boundary is set and the elements have been invoked, go to your central altar and light your central candle(s). Speak a short prayer to Vesta or the god or goddess you are honoring. For example:

"Vesta, keeper of the sacred flame,
I light this fire in your name.
Let it guard and bless this rite,
A beacon strong in sacred light."

The flame now serves as your witness and offering throughout the ritual. You may now also light a candle for the God and Goddess individually if you choose to. If you do, just ensure the focus flame remains directly in between them.

7.) Begin your spellwork

With the sacred boundary finally drawn, you may now proceed with any magical or devotional work. The boundary will hold steady as long as your attention and intention remain within it. If you step outside the boundary, pause and re-enter mindfully.

8.) Release the sacred boundary

When your ritual is complete, it is important to release the space with gratitude. Begin by speaking thanks to the gods and spirits for their attendance. If you invoked the four winds, thank and dismiss them one at a time as you extinguish the flames at each cardinal point. Then, extinguish the focus flame on your altar with care.

Next, walk the perimeter again, this time counterclockwise. As you walk, say:

> *"The rite is done, the space is clear,*
> *I thank the gods for being near.*
> *Let all return to what is right.*
> *The sacred rests, released to light."*

When you return to the east, pause, bow your head, and let the spiritual energy settle. The boundary is now released, and the space is returned to its ordinary state.

THE SACRED BOUNDARY is one of the most important elements in Roman Wiccan ritual. It is a declaration of purpose, a vessel of presence, and a shield of sanctity. Whether you are performing a simple devotional or a complex spell, take the time to memorize this ritual if you can. It will elevate your practice to a whole new level.

Journal Prompts

1.) Describe a moment when you instinctively knew you had entered sacred space. What senses alerted you?

2.) Plan your own version of this ritual, noting words, gestures, and physical markers you will employ to cast your sacred space.

3.) How might adopting the Roman concept of *pomerium* change the way you protect your energetic boundaries in daily life?

10

ASTROLOGY

Astrology in the ancient Roman world was not considered superstition; it was an essential part of civic and religious life. For those who are not familiar, astrology is the study of how celestial movements and positions may affect human affairs. The Romans inherited much of their celestial knowledge from the Greeks, who in turn had drawn from the Babylonians, but what Rome did best was *integrate*. They brought planetary worship into both public and private religion. Astrologers became prestigious consultants for the Roman emperor, using celestial birth charts to assess character, fate, and omens. Much of this has continued to live on in modern astrology and the *horoscope* as we know it today.

Each of the seven visible celestial bodies known to the Romans came to be associated with a deity. The Sun belonged to Sol, the Moon to Luna. The five wandering stars were identified with the gods Mercury, Venus, Mars, Jupiter, and Saturn. Each one had a distinct personality and ruled over a different aspect of life. It was believed that their positions and movements could influence everything from love and fortune to war and death.

Eventually these planetary deities became a major part of daily life. The Romans went so far as to name each day of the week after them, adjusting their calendar as a result. Sunday was the day of Sol. Monday was ruled by Luna. Tuesday belonged to Mars. Wednesday to Mercury. Thursday to Jupiter. Friday to Venus. Saturday to Saturn. This structure has survived all the way into the modern world, though many people no longer recognize the deity names behind the days.

Like the Roman pantheon of gods, each of the seven planetary deities governs a particular kind of energy:

Sol brings clarity, vitality, truth, and illumination. He is the force behind confidence, visibility, and leadership.

Luna governs dreams, emotion, reflection, intuition, and protection. Her power is cyclical, flowing like tides through the body and mind.

Mars fuels action, courage, boundaries, and aggression. He is useful when you need to break through something or defend what is yours.

Mercury brings speed, wit, communication, and adaptability. He governs messages, commerce, and the clever use of words. Jupiter rules wisdom, expansion, law, and blessings. He is the planet of abundance and spiritual growth.

Venus is love, beauty, charm, seduction, and sweetness. Her influence helps anything you wish to attract or create with harmony.

Saturn is structure, time, discipline, endings, and boundaries. Though his power can feel heavy, it teaches patience, endurance, and maturity.

By learning the energy of each planet, you can time your spells and rituals in harmony with their movements. It is similar to planting seeds according to the seasons. There are days and hours that help a particular kind of magic grow stronger. When you time your working with the correct planetary influence, it can act like a second wind at your back, pushing your intention forward through invisible channels.

The most basic method of working with planetary timing is through the days of the week:

Sunday is the day of Sol, ideal for rituals involving confidence, clarity, and health.

Monday is Luna's, perfect for introspection, healing, or dreamwork.

Tuesday belongs to Mars and can be used for protection, courage, or breaking through obstacles.

Wednesday is ruled by Mercury and supports anything involving communication, writing, or travel.

Thursday, ruled by Jupiter, is a day for expansion, success, legal matters, and spiritual growth.

Friday is Venus's day, best for love, beauty, pleasure, and harmony.

Saturday, sacred to Saturn, can be used for banishing, boundaries, ending bad habits, or serious reflection.

You do not need to reshape your entire life around the planetary week to practice astrology as the Romans did. Even a small act of recognition, like lighting a gold candle on Sunday morning in honor of Sol, or writing in your dream journal on a Monday night with Luna in mind, can deepen your connection. It is a way of remembering that the sacred moves through time as well as space. Over time, you may begin to notice that each day of the week carries unique emotions. Some may feel light and social. Others may feel quiet or restrained. You are just beginning to feel how these currents flow throughout the week.

For more precise timing, you can learn to work with planetary hours. Each day is divided into twelve parts between sunrise and sunset, with another twelve from sunset to sunrise. Each hour is ruled by a planet, following a repeating sequence. The first hour after sunrise is always ruled by the planet that governs the day. So on Friday, the first hour is ruled by Venus. From there, the cycle continues in this traditional order: Saturn, Jupiter, Mars, Sol, Venus, Mercury, Luna, and so on. There are many tools available online to help you calculate these hours for your exact location. If you are preparing a spell or ritual that requires precision, choosing the right planetary hour can increase its effectiveness.

Working with planetary hours does not have to become a burden. Even if you do not calculate them daily, you may still choose to cast a charm during the hour of Mercury on a Wednesday afternoon, or to burn a protective herb during the hour of Mars on Tuesday evening. These small adjustments help tune your actions to the right frequency.

In addition to timing your work, you can also create physical connections to the planets through tools, colors, and symbols. On your altar, you might include a golden disk for Sol, a silver bowl of water for Luna, a red stone for Mars, a feather or coin for Mercury, a sprig of oak for Jupiter, a rose quartz or seashell for Venus, and a piece of obsidian or dark wood for Saturn. These items do not need to be elaborate or expensive, so long as they feel meaningful to you.

If you are more interested in personal growth and development, your birth chart can be used to discover which planetary forces are strong or weak within you. Even if you are not an experienced astrologer, discovering your rising sign will at least reveal which planet rules your chart. This ruling planet often reflects your overall energy and may become a personal ally in magical work. If your rising sign is Aries, Mars becomes your guide. If it is Cancer, Luna takes that role. Pay attention to how this planet shows up in your life.

You may feel its pull more strongly or experience lessons tied to its domain.

The best way to practice planetary magic as the Romans did is to live with it. Begin by observing. Keep a small journal and write down your thoughts, dreams, and moods each day, noting which planetary day it is. Then, watch for patterns, especially in the sky. Is Venus shining brightly in the west after sunset? Is Saturn rising before dawn? Let these observations deepen your connection. Over time, you may feel that the planets call to you in ritual. Lean into these forces and see what you can learn from them.

Journal Prompts

1.) Chart a recent decision you made and examine how planetary archetypes might have influenced it.

2.) Compare the Roman view of celestial order with your personal belief about fate versus free will.

3.) Identify one planetary deity you rarely consider. Research its qualities and record how welcoming that influence might broaden your perspective.

11

HARUSPICY

The Romans believed that the gods could speak through auspicious signs in nature. Among the most respected and fearsome forms of divination was *haruspicy*, the practice of examining the entrails of sacrificed animals to determine the favor or displeasure of the gods. It was a sacred art passed down through generations, requiring thorough training and ritual precision.

The word haruspicy comes from the Etruscan roots of Roman religion, originating long before the Republic was founded. The *haruspex*, or diviner, was a priest trained to read omens in the livers, lungs, and hearts of animals, most often sheep or bulls. These were carefully conducted rites performed before important public events, including wars, treaties, temple dedications, or decisions of great political consequence. The fate of Rome could hang on what was found in the body of a single animal.

The most sacred organ was the liver. It was believed to be the seat of life and divine communication. Haruspices would examine the shape, color, texture, and position of its lobes. They would note any marks, holes, or unusual features, comparing them to detailed models kept for instruction. Some of these models survive to this day, such as the famous *Liver of Piacenza*, marked with the names of gods and divided into regions like a celestial map. In this way, the liver was seen as a reflection of the heavens. The gods wrote their will upon it as if it were a scroll of flesh.

Haruspicy was often used alongside augury, another Roman divinatory system that involved watching the flight of birds (see chapter 16). Augury dealt with signs in the sky, while haruspicy looked beneath the earth, into the hidden workings of the body. Together, they formed a complete vision of heaven and earth speaking in harmony. To ignore either was seen as dangerous and foolhardy.

To be clear, the practice was not a simple matter of yes or no. Haruspices were trained to interpret nuance, to understand how divine displeasure might be partial, or how a seemingly favorable omen might carry hidden warnings. A blemish in one section of the liver could signal danger in a specific part of the undertaking. A missing lobe might suggest that an essential element had been over-looked. Sometimes a new sacrifice had to be made if the signs were unclear. The gods were not always easy to read.

Though the practice began with the Etruscans, it was fully embraced by the Romans. Even when more Hellenistic forms of divination gained popularity, haruspicy remained a powerful institu-tion. The Senate maintained official *haruspices* to advise on public matters. Emperors kept private diviners to interpret omens. In times of crisis, it was often the *haruspex* who was called upon to make sense of the chaos.

The logic behind this practice might seem foreign to us now, but it was rooted in a Roman worldview where everything was intercon-nected. The health of the animal reflected the health of the act it was meant to sanctify. If the gods withdrew their blessing, it would show in the organs. Sacrifice was not just about giving something to the divine. It was a conversation, an inquiry, and a revelation. When the haruspex opened the body, he was opening a path between worlds.

In modern practice, we do not need to replicate the literal rites of haruspicy to draw meaning from them. Most practitioners today do not sacrifice animals, but the symbolic power of this act still offers wisdom. The lesson of haruspicy is this: there is no clear divide between the physical and the spiritual. The body speaks. The world reflects hidden truths. What matters most lies just beneath the surface.

You might translate this into your own rituals through symbolic observation. When performing a sacrifice of food, herbs, or candles, observe how they behave. Does the flame flicker? Does the offering burn cleanly or give off smoke? Do patterns appear in the wax or ash? These are subtle forms of reading, drawing from the same spirit of divination. You are watching for the voice of the divine to emerge from the ordinary.

Another way to honor the spirit of haruspicy is through anatomical meditation. Focus on your own body as a temple. Each heartbeat, breath, or ache can reveal something about your internal world. If the gods once wrote their signs in the organs of animals, perhaps they still whisper through your blood and bones. Pay attention to what your body is trying to tell you. Illness, tension, or sudden emotion can act as signals from the divine.

You might also incorporate symbolic tools to represent the organs once studied. On your altar, you could place a liver-shaped stone or a sculpted model, using it as a focus for divination or as a place to petition the gods for insight. Write your question on a slip of paper and tuck it beneath the object. Leave an offering, then return the next day to read the patterns in the wax, the smoke, or your own dreams. Let the practice evolve in a way that honors the old without needing to reenact it exactly.

If you feel called to more direct forms of divination, consider using a set of casting bones, runes, or marked stones as your modern equivalent. These items fall into similar patterns. They land in ways that seem random, but often echo deeper truths. Each bone, like each lobe of the liver, can represent a different aspect of life.

To read the signs is to listen. To ask the gods for guidance is to admit that your own knowledge has limits. There is a quiet strength in this. The ancient haruspex stood at the threshold between human will and divine law, between flesh and fate. That role remains as powerful today as it was two thousand years ago.

Journal Prompts

1.) Reflect on a time you "read signs" in everyday life (cloud shapes, tea leaves, coincidences). What message did you take?

2.) How do you reconcile intuitive divination with analytical reasoning? Journal about achieving balance between them.

3.) Draft a symbolic, ethical version of haruspicy that respects the ancient tradition while suiting contemporary practice.

12

DEFIXIONES

Not all Roman magic had good intentions. While much of Roman religious life focused on maintaining peace with the gods and seeking blessings from the divine, there was also a darker side. These were the practices of cursing, binding, and calling upon unseen forces to influence others in secret. Among the most iconic examples of this were the *defixiones*, thin sheets of lead or pewter inscribed with curses, folded or pierced, and hidden away in places of power. They were the curse tablets of Rome, used to seek justice, vengeance, or control.

The word *defixio* comes from the Latin verb *defigere*, meaning to fasten or to bind. That is exactly what these spells intended to do. They were designed to bind a person's actions, speech, or success, often in highly specific ways. Many of them were found nailed to temple walls, buried in graves, or thrown into sacred springs, where they would be carried into the underworld by water or sealed by the dead. These locations were not chosen randomly. They were considered thresholds between the human world and the spiritual realm— places where messages could pass between dimensions.

Curse tablets were used by all types of Roman citizens who felt wronged, overlooked, or desperate. A merchant might use a defixio against a rival to ruin his business. A lover might try to curse the person who stole their beloved. Athletes were even known to curse their opponents before games in hopes of sabotaging their performance.

The structure of a defixio was usually simple. It began by naming the person to be cursed, often including multiple identifying details, in order to ensure the magic reached the right target. This was followed by a specific list of what the curser wanted to happen. A thief might be bound from speaking or sleeping until they confessed. A rival might be blinded, silenced, or driven to ruin. The more precise the language, the more potent the spell was believed to be. Some even included drawings of the victim or symbols meant to amplify the binding.

Next came the invocation of spiritual forces. These might include chthonic deities, the dead, or even spirits of vengeance. Pluto, Proserpina, Hecate, and the Manes were commonly called upon. These were entities of the underworld, capable of acting on darker desires. The tone of the tablet was often demanding. Rather than praying for justice, the writer commanded the spirits to act on their behalf, even threatening them with punishment if they failed to obey.

Once written, the tablet was usually folded, rolled, or pierced with nails to physically represent the binding. It might then be hidden in a grave, dropped into a well, or buried at a crossroads. Each of these locations was chosen for its liminal nature—its nearness to the spirit world. By placing the curse in these spaces, the writer hoped to send their message directly into the hands of unseen forces, bypassing the need for ritual or ceremony.

It is easy to think of these acts as cruel, but many defixiones read less like acts of vengeance and more like cries for help. A woman begs the gods to return her stolen clothing. A child pleads for revenge on a man who wronged her mother. A shopkeeper asks for justice after being cheated by a customer. The line between magic and law was thin in the Roman world. If the courts could not provide justice, perhaps the spirits would.

Today, hundreds of defixiones have been recovered by archaeologists, mostly in the western provinces of the Roman Empire. Many were found in Britain, especially at the sacred spring in Bath, where the goddess Sulis Minerva was worshipped. Inscriptions there range from petty grievances to serious curses. One tablet reads, "*Docimedis has lost two gloves. May he who has stolen them lose his mind and his eyes in the temple where she appoints.*" Others are more poetic or obscure, written in spirals or backwards letters to add magical force.

If you wish to explore the defixio in your own practice, it should be approached with care and ethical thought. Modern practitioners sometimes adapt this form not to curse others, but to bind harmful patterns, silence negative self-talk, or remove toxic influences from their lives. The ritual act of writing a problem down, naming it fully, and then sealing it away can be a powerful way to let go of pain or restore your own sense of justice.

To create your own version of a defixio, begin by clearly stating what needs to be bound or released. Use precise language. The act of naming gives power to the spell. Then write this intention on a piece of thin metal, parchment, or even paper, if traditional materials are unavailable. You may wish to call upon protective spirits or ancestors to witness the act and ensure it is just. Once complete, fold or pierce the tablet and bury it in a safe and appropriate place. This could be near a natural boundary, like a riverbank, or within a sacred container on your altar.

Remember that Roman magic works under the principle of divine reciprocity. If you ask the dead or the gods to act on your behalf, you must be prepared to give something in return. This might be a coin, a candle, or a vow to restore balance once justice is served. The principle of *do ut des* still applies. You give so that the divine may give in return.

There is power in speaking what is unspeakable. There is strength in writing what cannot be said aloud. The curse tablets of ancient Rome are true testaments to the innate human desire for justice. With this power, however, comes immense responsibility. Make sure you always conduct your spellwork with good intentions.

Journal Prompts

1.) Explore your feelings about curses or binding spells. Where is your personal moral line?

2.) Write about a situation where speech or writing felt as potent as magic, either for harm or for healing.

3.) Consider how you might transmute anger or injustice into a protective spell rather than a harmful one.

13

THE BULLA

The *bulla* was a small amulet worn around the neck of young Roman boys as a symbol of protection and divine favor. Though often associated with children, the bulla held deep meaning across Roman society, bridging the realms of family, magic, and fate.

A Roman child received their bulla on the day of their birth or shortly after, typically during a naming ceremony known as the *dies lustricus*. This day marked the child's formal entrance into society. The bulla was placed around their neck by the father or guardian, often with a prayer for safety and long life. From that moment on, it was never to be removed in public. It marked the wearer as protected and watched over, both by the household gods and by the ancestors who stood behind the family line.

The shape of the bulla varied, but it was usually a rounded or heart-shaped locket, made from gold, leather, or cloth depending on the family's wealth. Inside it were placed small charms, herbs, or written prayers—anything thought to guard the child from harm. Chief among these dangers was the *evil eye*, a malicious force believed to be cast through envy or ill will. The Romans believed children were especially vulnerable to this kind of spiritual attack. Their innocence, beauty, or good fortune could attract unseen dangers. The bulla acted as a shield, turning away ill intent before it could settle.

For boys, the bulla also carried a civic meaning. It was worn until the day they came of age and assumed the toga *virilis*, symbolizing their entrance into manhood. On that day, the bulla was ritually removed and often dedicated to the household gods. This act marked the transition from childhood to citizen. It was a rite of passage, separating the protected world of the family from the public duties of Roman life. For girls, the bulla might be worn until marriage, when it was either set aside or replaced by new symbols of adulthood.

Though the bulla began as a child's charm, its essence was magical. It created a liminal space around the wearer, a personal sanctuary that followed them through the world. It was charged with intention and belief. Some families passed down *bullae* (multiple amulets) across generations, turning them into heirlooms. Others were buried with their owners, ensuring that the protection they offered in life would continue in the afterlife.

The magic of the bulla was closely tied to the *Lares* and *Penates*, the household spirits that guarded the family line. To wear a bulla was to walk in the circle of their protection. It was a daily offering, worn over the heart as a symbol of sacred connection.

In modern spiritual practice, the concept of the bulla remains highly relevant. Many practitioners of Wicca craft their own protective amulets, designed to guard against negative energy, psychic attack, or spiritual unrest. Whether worn as necklaces, carried in pockets, or kept on altars, these charms can carry real spiritual significance if made with proper intention.

You can make your own modern bulla using any materials that speak to you. Choose a small pouch, locket, or container that can be worn or kept close. Fill it with items of protective significance. This might include a pinch of salt, a piece of black tourmaline, a written charm, or a strand of hair from a loved one. The exact contents do not matter as much as their meaning. What matters is that they are chosen with a specific intention in mind.

Once your bulla is assembled, take time to charge it through ritual. You might hold it over incense smoke, pass it through candle-light, or speak a protective prayer while holding it against your chest. Ask your ancestors, spirits, or chosen deities to bless it. Then wear it, especially during times when you feel vulnerable or spiritually exposed. It is a reminder that you are not unguarded. You have a spiritual network here to help you.

Some practitioners create bullae for specific purposes. One may be designed to protect against envy or gossip. Another may shield the heart during grief or emotional upheaval. You might even make bullae for children, friends, or loved ones, just as the Romans did. These gifts can carry deep meaning. They are living prayers offered in the form of an object.

You can also include a bulla on your altar. Treat it as a focal point of household protection. Offer candles or incense near it. Whisper to it when you feel afraid. The physical presence of the bulla gives shape to your inner strength. Over time, it will carry the weight of your prayers, absorbing the energy of every moment you reach for it.

Even if you never wear a physical charm, you can still carry this mindset. Let your daily practices become your bulla. Let your morning ritual be a spiritual necklace you put on to face the world. Let your prayers become invisible armor. The lesson of the bulla is that protection is not found in one object alone. It is found in the unseen web of sacred connection that we tend each day.

The Roman bulla may have been small, but its presence was mighty. It guarded the hearts of children, linked the living to the dead, and made divine protection something you could feel against your skin. It reminds us even now that magic doesn't have to be dramatic. Sometimes the most powerful spells are quiet and worn close to the heart.

Journal Prompts

I.) Recall or imagine a protective charm from your childhood. What meaning did it hold then and now?

2.) Sketch a modern bulla design incorporating symbols of personal resilience.

3.) Reflect on the threshold moments (birthdays, graduations, job interviews) when you felt the need for extra protection. How can ritual objects support such transitions?

SECTION III:
THE PRIESTHOOD

Roman religion was highly structured, with priesthoods responsible for maintaining a sacred order. In this section, we will explore each of these roles and reinterpret them for a Wiccan coven. You will see how the historical offices of the Flamen, Pontifex, Augur, and Vestal can each be transformed into archetypes for magical leadership.

14

CONCERNING COVENS

Wiccans are no strangers to covens. For many of us, it was our coven that first introduced us to ritual and seasonal celebration. Even those who walk a solitary path understand the value of this collective power. In traditional Wicca, covens are often structured around degrees of initiation, led by a High Priestess and High Priest, and organized around a symbolic balance of feminine and masculine forces. This system works beautifully, and for many, it is enough... but what if you want to root your coven in Roman tradition?

This provides an opportunity to rethink coven structure using the spiritual roles and priesthoods of Ancient Rome as inspiration. Just as Wicca draws from the ceremonial, folkloric, and esoteric traditions of Europe, Roman Wicca can draw from the sacred offices of the Roman world—roles like the Flamen, Augur, Pontifex, and Vestal. They represent distinct spiritual responsibilities, each with its own form of knowledge, training, and ritual authority.

In a Roman Wiccan coven, leadership and roles do not need to follow the traditional Wiccan model of High Priest and Priestess. Instead, a coven may be organized more like a college of priests, where each person embodies a sacred function rooted in Roman spiritual philosophy. There is still structure. There are still rites of passage. But the focus shifts from polarity-based leadership to role-based service. Each member becomes a vessel for a specific aspect of sacred work.

This does not mean throwing away the Wiccan framework. We are just adapting to it. The core values remain: balance, intention, initiation, ritual, and the turning of the year. What changes is the imagery, the language, and the spiritual roles we step into. By drawing from Roman priesthoods, we gain access to a new symbolic structure that carries real historical weight.

Going forward, the chapters in this section will outline a suggested model for coven hierarchy using Roman religious archetypes. Each chapter will explore a specific role and its unique responsibilities within the coven as a whole. There are four different roles a coven member may step into:

The **Flamen** acts as the ritual priest, leading formal rites and tending the coven's relationship with specific deities through devotionals.

The **Augur** serves as the interpreter of omens and signs, helping guide the coven through divination magic and spiritual insight.

The **Pontifex** acts as a governing body for the coven, maintaining its calendar, ethics, and ritual standards. You can think of this as a High Priest or Priestess of sorts.

The **Vestal** tends the sacred flame and upholds the spiritual purity and sanctity of the group space. Their focus is on cleansing and protection magic.

Keep in mind that these roles are just starting points. A coven can use all of them, some of them, or adapt them to fit the unique needs of the group. They may also exist alongside familiar Wiccan roles like Maiden, Crone, and Guardian. This makes it less of a replacement and more of an expansion.

If you are already in a coven, these roles may help deepen and refine your structure. If you are starting a new group, they can provide a strong foundation to build upon. Even if you are a solitary practitioner, they may still serve as archetypes for your own spiritual development, helping you clarify your magical strengths and areas of weakness.

Most importantly, a Roman Wiccan coven is *not* about strict hierarchy. It is about sacred function and collaborative governance. Each role reflects a relationship with divine power that are all equally important. Just as unique gods come together to form a pantheon, a coven is strongest when each member brings something different to the group.

Journal Prompts

1.) What roles or structures help a spiritual group thrive? List qualities you would seek or provide in your own coven.

2.) Write about your past teamwork experiences. Which aspects felt sacred, and which disrupted harmony?

15

THE FLAMEN

In the religious world of Ancient Rome, the *flamen* was a priest of the gods. They were an official of high sanctity, personally bound to a specific deity through ritual, clothing, and daily practice. There were many types of flamines, but each served a specific god or goddess with unbroken devotion. They oversaw sacrifices, maintained temple rites, and ensured that the divine favor remained steady through proper observance. In Rome, the favor of the gods had to be cultivated through ongoing service, and the flamen stood at the very center of that important and sacred relationship.

The word *flamen* itself has uncertain origins, though many linguists associate it with an archaic root linked to "burning" or "blazing," likely referencing their role in offering fire-sacrifices to the gods. Others suggest connections to *flo-* or *flare*, linking it to speech or invocation. Regardless of etymology, the flamen was both the speaker and the steward, someone who bridged the physical world and divine realm through ritual accuracy and personal sanctity. Their position was not symbolic. It was considered vital to the spiritual health of the Roman state.

The most important among the flamines were the three *flamines maiores*: the Flamen Dialis, Flamen Martialis, and Flamen Quirinalis, who served Jupiter, Mars, and Quirinus respectively. These roles were highly regulated. The Flamen Dialis, in particular, was subject to dozens of arbitrary ritual restrictions. His hair and nails could only be cut under auspicious signs, and he was not permitted to ride a horse, touch metal, or even swear oaths. These prohibitions were meant to reinforce his sacral status and symbolized his complete dedication to the god Jupiter.

His wife, the *Flaminica Dialis*, was also a priestess in her own right. The couple could only be married by a Pontifex Maximus in a ceremony called *confarreatio*, which involved the sharing of sacred spelt bread. If the Flaminica died, the Flamen Dialis was forced to resign. Together, they formed a living expression of devotion to their god, and their lives became a constant act of worship. For modern practitioners of Wicca, such intense restrictions are obviously impractical, however, the spirit behind them is still meaningful.

In the context of Roman Wicca, the flamen becomes the primary ritualist of the coven. They are responsible for preparing, organizing, and leading group ceremonies, particularly those aligned with a specific deity. Unlike the High Priest or Priestess, who may oversee all rites equally, the flamen may be dedicated to a single god or goddess and serve as their spokesperson and devotee. This means that in some covens, multiple flamines may exist, each serving a distinct divine power.

If your coven is small or newly forming, one person may serve as a flamen for the entire group. This is perfectly acceptable, especially if you are only working with one or two gods. A flamen must also know the rites of their coven well. They should be familiar with the deity's mythology, ancient offerings, planetary correspondences, and preferred sacred symbols. They should be able to mark a sacred boundary from memory and be able to invoke divine forces with confidence and clarity.

This is why daily devotional practice is so critical for someone in this role. You cannot expect to call a god or goddess into your space if you have made no effort to build a relationship with them. A flamen should pray regularly to their deity, tend to a shrine, and offer small gifts even outside of ritual settings. This is how trust is formed and how you learn to listen. If at any point during a ritual you feel awkward calling on a deity, it most certainly means your relationship is not strong enough yet.

Historical records tell us that the Flamen Dialis offered a daily sacrifice of bread and wine to Jupiter at dawn. He observed lunar phases carefully and participated in key state rituals tied to agriculture, justice, and civic blessing. His very presence was believed to bring sanctity to the spaces he entered. While such formality is not required in Wicca, the flamen should still approach their practice with consistency and reverence. Perhaps you light a candle for your god each morning or speak their name before meals. You can even prepare offerings in private before the coven comes together to save the group time. These acts do not need to be dramatic. They will work as long as they are sincere.

When preparing a coven ritual, the flamen is responsible for establishing the sacred boundary, invoking the appropriate deity, and guiding the group through the structure of the rite. This includes organizing any libations, preparing a patera or simpulum for offerings, and ensuring that the timing of the ritual aligns with the god's nature or known feast day. For example, a Flamen of Mars might time ritual for Tuesdays. A Flamen of Vesta may prefer rites held in the morning, with fire-based offerings in alignment with the practices of Vestalia. You will have to research your patron deity in more detail to discover these quirks for yourself.

It is important to note that ancient flamines did not work alone. They were part of a broader religious network of augurs, pontiffs, and other priesthoods. Thus, it's vital that the flamen learn to work collaboratively with others. If the augur is guiding a divination ritual, the flamen ensures the space is ritually prepared. If the pontifex is setting the coven calendar, the flamen may consult on the appropriate rites for the year ahead. This model is not top-down. It is collaborative.

Some groups may choose to formally initiate someone into the role of flamen. If so, the ritual should involve a public dedication to the deity being served. The person might be asked to compose a personal prayer, present a handmade offering, or speak about their relationship with the god. They may then be given a ritual tool associated with their service, such as a patera, a flame, a colored sash, or necklace. From that point on, they take on the sacred duty of keeping that deity present in the life of the coven.

The title is not what makes the flamen. It is the daily work. It is the way they prepare the ritual space with care and speak a deity's name with clarity. It is the way they show up for the group and hold space when others are grieving, angry, confused, or tired. The flamen do not have the most dramatic job, but they are dependable. They show up, again and again, with their offerings and their presence. That constancy becomes power.

In Ancient Rome, the role of flamen was considered lifelong. One did not resign unless forced to by death or disqualification. In our world, such permanence may not be possible. People move and life often changes. But if you take on this role, understand the seriousness of what it asks. You are stepping into a lineage of spiritual service that is over two thousand years old. Your work is now responsible for preserving that legacy.

Even if you are a solitary practitioner, the role of flamen can still be meaningful. You may become the ritualist for your home, for your ancestors, or for your personal pantheon. You may lead rites during the Roman festivals, invoke the gods in your own space, and become a steward of divine presence in the world. Whether done in private or in public, the task remains the same: to keep the connection between humanity and divinity strong, intentional, and alive.

Journal Prompts

1.) Identify an area of expertise you could tend with the dedication of a flamen. How would daily practice look?

2.) Write about the relationship between ritual duty and personal identity in your life.

3.) Envision a vow you might take to uphold a specific spiritual or communal responsibility.

16

THE AUGUR

The augur specializes in intuitive magic and divination, often receiving messages from the gods through nature. While the flamen conduct rituals and maintain an ongoing relationship with the gods, the augur's task is to observe, interpret, and declare whether a given action had the gods' blessing. In other words, an augur can help determine if an act of magic was successful or if a relationship with a deity is in turmoil.

Nothing of civic or religious importance in Rome was to proceed without first seeking the wisdom of the auspices. A temple could not be built, a battle could not be launched, and a magistrate could not assume office until the augur had confirmed that the omens were favorable. In essence, the augur functioned as the voice of the gods for the people.

The practice of augury was rooted in intuitive observation of the natural world. The augur did not predict the future in the way modern people might imagine a seer or oracle doing. Instead, they determined whether or not the gods would approve of a planned action via a yes or no answer observed through signs in nature. The most traditional form involved marking out a sacred quadrant of sky, called a *templum,* and then watching the behavior of birds within that space. The type of bird, its direction of flight, whether it made a sound, and how many were seen all carried symbolic meaning. The results were interpreted according to established custom and delivered as a judgment of divine approval or disapproval. This was actually considered a formal religious science, backed by tradition and rigorous training.

The word auspices, derived from auspex or "bird-watcher," reflects how central birds were to the practice, but the signs used in augury extended beyond avian behavior. Lightning, cloud patterns, sudden animal appearances, and natural phenomena like earthquakes or falling objects could all carry meaning if witnessed within the proper context.

Inaugurations, dedications, military marches, and sacrifices all required this kind of divinatory confirmation, which made the augur one of the most respected and necessary figures in Roman public life. Though augury began as a religious art practiced by the priesthood, over time it became a political role as well. The power to declare divine favor, or to delay a decision by citing unfavorable omens, was a potent form of spiritual authority.

In Roman Wicca, the augur takes on a similar function, serving as the diviner of the group. Rather than predicting the distant future, the augur in a coven reads the signs of the present moment to determine whether the timing, alignment, or intent of a working is in harmony with the divine. This can be done in a variety of ways and can include as much or as little Roman tradition as you like. One augur may use birdwatching and celestial observation in the traditional Roman manner, while another might prefer modern divinatory tools such as tarot, runes, pendulums, or astrology. The methods may differ, but the underlying function remains: to discern the will of the gods and guide magical workings to success.

What separates the augur from a casual diviner is not the complexity of their tools, but the discipline and integrity of their approach. The augur does not seek signs in order to satisfy curiosity or gain personal advantage. They are not trying to manipulate fate or impress others with predictions. Instead, they are asking the world a question and waiting to receive an answer that may or may not align with their desires. The augur must be willing to see clearly and speak honestly. If the signs point to delay, they must say so. If the gods seem silent, they must admit uncertainty. This is not an easy task, especially in a group setting where others may be eager to proceed with plans. The augur protects the integrity of the work by ensuring that it aligns with something greater than human will.

In the context of a coven, the augur often works closely with the flamen. Before any major ritual or festival, the augur may be asked to take the auspices or perform a divination to determine whether the timing and intention are in spiritual harmony. If something feels off or the energy of the group is unsettled, then they may advise postponement or adjustment. It's important to note that the augur is not above other coven members in authority, but they do serve a unique function that supports the entire group. Their role is protective, not controlling, and their responsibility is to the gods and the truth of what they see.

Modern augurs may also find value in studying natural rhythms from a scientific perspective. The moon phases, planetary transits, solstices, equinoxes, tides, and seasonal shifts all carry spiritual information. A storm on the day of a planned ritual may be an omen to postpone. A dream that recurs the night before a major spell may be a warning. The augur learns to notice these patterns with careful attention and finds effective ways to communicate it to the rest of the group.

In Ancient Rome, augurs were formally trained and often came from wealthy patrician families, but modern practitioners do not require any sort of bloodline to walk this path. The qualities that matter most are patience, discernment, and a willingness to remain grounded in the face of adversity. The augur must not fall into sensationalism or claim to know more than they do. A quiet, thoughtful reading that admits its limitations is far more powerful than one that forces a narrative onto unclear signs. In fact, restraint is one of the augur's greatest virtues. The gods speak in the language of subtlety. A sudden breeze, a missing candle, or a hawk overhead are the kinds of signs that will speak if the augur is listening.

Some covens may choose to initiate someone into the role of augur through a formal inauguration, perhaps by asking them to observe a ritual and offer a divinatory reading before the group. They may be given a lituus or other divinatory tool that they consecrate themselves while pledging to their role as augur. The details are not important, as long as the intention is sincere. You can initiate in any way your coven sees fit.

Even if you practice alone without a coven, you can still become an augur. Each morning you might step outside, face the sky, and ask for guidance. Over time, you will learn what the world looks like when the gods are pleased and what it looks like when something is out of alignment. These patterns will not reveal themselves all at once. They build slowly, through repeated observation and careful reflection. The more you listen, the more you will begin to hear.

As you can see, the augur was extremely important to Roman society, and you can use this role in your own coven to add extra spiritual weight to your rituals. You will have to decide for yourselves what natural occurrences correspond to which messages. They may come through birds, weather, dreams, tarot, or just about anything else. The augur just has to be willing to observe, interpret, and offer what they see.

Journal Prompts

1.) Describe a recent omen you noticed in nature and the insight it offered.

2.) How can cultivating patience enhance your ability to read subtle signs? Draft a plan to slow down and observe.

3.) Write about the ethical considerations of sharing divinatory messages with others. Should you share a reading with someone if the outcome looks bad?

17

THE PONTIFEX

The office of the pontifex was the most powerful position within the Roman priesthood. Unlike the flamen or augur, whose duties centered on specific deities or ritual events, the pontifex was responsible for maintaining the overall structure, integrity, and legal oversight of Roman religion. The term *pontifex* is often translated as "bridge-builder," a name that speaks symbolically to their role as a mediator between the mortal and divine worlds. They were architects of ritual law, keepers of the sacred calendar, and custodians of tradition. No religious system survives without structure, and it was the pontiffs who ensured that order was preserved.

The *Collegium Pontificum*, or College of Pontiffs, was the governing body of Roman religion. It included several members of varying ranks, with the *Pontifex Maximus* at its head. This high priest was considered the supreme religious authority in Rome, overseeing public rites, sacred law, the regulation of priesthoods, and the formal recognition of new cults or temples. The pontiffs managed the religious calendar, kept track of feast days and intercalary months, and ensured that no ritual was performed outside of its proper time. They also recorded precedents and decisions in annalistic form, creating a long-standing legal memory for religious practice.

In the early Republic, the Pontifex Maximus was elected and held office for life. Over time, the role became politically charged. Julius Caesar famously held the title before becoming dictator, and subsequent emperors adopted it as part of their authority. The fusion of spiritual and political power gave the office extraordinary influence. Even when the emperor was not personally performing rites, the title of Pontifex Maximus served to legitimize his role as the ultimate guardian of Roman religion.

The duties of the pontiffs were practical and administrative, but they were never merely bureaucratic. These priests served as the central authority on matters of ritual purity, sacrificial law, inheritance of priesthoods, and the boundaries of public and private religious obligations. They ensured that rituals were correct not only in their form, but also in their timing, sequence, and theological context. If a mistake was made during a sacrifice, the pontiffs would have final say whether the rite needed to be repeated, amended, or dismissed. Their decisions were binding, and their knowledge of sacred protocol was thought to be unmatched.

In Roman Wicca, the pontifex can serve a parallel function within the coven. While the flamen conducts rites and the augur reads signs, it is the pontifex who maintains the governing structure of the group. They ensure that the ritual calendar is respected, that the coven's practices remain internally consistent, and that the evolving body of work is preserved in a way that can be safely archived for generations. They are the keeper of tradition, the codifier of the group's shared theology, and the one who steps in when clarity is needed on what is appropriate or out of alignment.

The pontifex knows the dates of every major festival and ensures that preparations begin in time. They are familiar with the sacred texts, prayers, and liturgies used by the group, and they make sure that no rite becomes distorted through neglect or misremembering. If a new member joins the coven, it is often the pontifex who introduces them to the foundational practices, ensuring they understand not only the *how*, but also the *why*.

In a coven where multiple flamines or augurs may be present, the pontifex becomes the axis around which these roles are coordinated. They may determine who leads which rite, when a certain deity is honored, and how the group collectively approaches seasonal observances. If a question arises about the ethics of a certain spell or the spiritual implications of a divinatory message, the pontifex helps guide that conversation toward consensus and balance.

Because of the nature of this work, the pontifex must have a strong foundation in religious history, magical theory, and spiritual ethics. Their authority comes from years of study and lived experience. They are the scholar-practitioner of the group, able to cite historical precedent and articulate the theological rationale behind certain choices. In this way, the pontifex helps ground the coven in a well-informed and structured framework of practice.

This does not have to mean rigidity or resistance to change. The historical pontiffs were capable of adapting practice when needed, especially when confronted with new cults or social shifts. They understood that religion *must* remain relevant to the people it serves. Thus, a coven's pontifex should be open to evolution, but always rooted in a strong foundation of tradition.

To act as pontifex is also to act as historian. The group's rites, prayers, and observations should be written down and preserved into a grimoire. If a new ritual is created, the pontifex ensures that it is documented and reviewed. If a festival is celebrated with unique customs or significant events, those experiences are recorded so that future members can understand how the group evolved.

This role may also extend into training. If the coven has degrees or initiatory levels, the pontifex may be responsible for designing the curriculum, overseeing advancement, or conducting certain initiations. Their knowledge of the broader religious framework ensures that new practitioners are not simply memorizing scripts, but internalizing the deeper purpose behind the tradition. They help others grow into their roles by teaching the structure behind rituals that allows magic to really work.

While the flamen calls down the gods and the augur listens to their will, the pontifex ensures that the temple stands and the scrolls are legible. It is a leadership role with deep responsibility, akin to the High Priest or Priestess within a coven. It is less visible in ritual but equally essential. Without a pontifex, a coven may begin to fray at the edges. Rituals become inconsistent, dates are missed, and traditions are slowly forgotten. The pontifex exists to prevent that erosion and protect the integrity of the practice, even if other members get lazy or complacent.

Some covens may formally recognize the pontifex through a rite of initiation, perhaps involving the presentation of a ritual calendar, a scroll, or a ceremonial garment. The person chosen should have proven themselves capable of long-term dedication, clear thought, and respectful leadership. The role should not be taken on lightly. In fact, you may want to hold a vote to select your pontifex as a community. A good pontifex does not seek attention and wants only for the coven to thrive.

If you feel called to this role, begin by studying the old Roman calendars. Learn the Roman festivals and the rites tied to the gods you honor. Write down some rituals and begin to organize notes for your coven. Begin to understand how structure creates freedom, and how consistency creates depth. When you build your practice with this extra level of care, the gods *will* notice.

Journal Prompts

1.) Examine your current "spiritual calendar." What rhythms or holy days need clearer structure?

2.) Reflect on the bridges you have built between people, ideas, or worlds in your own life.

3.) Outline steps to safeguard sacred law or tradition in your practice while still allowing evolution.

18

THE VESTAL

The vestals were priestesses of Vesta, a Roman goddess of hearth and ritual purity. As guardians of the eternal flame, these women held one of the most prestigious roles in Roman society. Their primary duty was to keep the sacred fire burning in the Temple of Vesta, a flame believed to ensure the continued life and protection of the Roman state. If the fire were to extinguish, it was considered a sign that Rome itself was falling out of divine favor. To prevent this, the vestals maintained constant care over the space, ensuring the flame was kept lit at all times.

The Temple of Vesta was oddly shaped compared to other temples at the time. It was round like a hearth, open to the sky, and accessible to the public only during the sacred festival of Vestalia. The flame within it was tended with utmost precision. The vestals swept the floors daily, removed ashes, washed the altar stones, and purified the space with water drawn from sacred springs. Every part of their daily work reinforced the spiritual order that made Roman rites possible.

In Wicca, the vestal can be reimagined as the coven's purifier and space-keeper. The modern vestal is a master of protection magic,

ensuring every ritual environment is cleansed physically and spiritually before others arrive. They cleanse the altar, sweep the floor, light
the candles, and mark the sacred boundary. They burn purifying
herbs like rosemary, hyssop, or bay leaf to remove stagnant energy.

This role is central to the success of ritual. If the space is not properly cleansed and centered, then any magical working performed
within it becomes unstable. The boundaries of the circle may be
weak. The focus of the group may scatter. The presence of the gods
may feel distant or dulled. Sacred space must be cultivated with
intention, and the vestal ensures that it is done properly.

Preparing the space begins well before the ritual itself. The vestal
often arrives first, unlocking the door or opening the outdoor site.
They may set up the altar, arrange tools, and lay out offerings. They
inspect candles to ensure they are trimmed and steady. If there is
debris, it is cleared away. If the energy feels heavy or chaotic, they
perform a quiet cleansing rite. This might involve sprinkling consecrated water around the perimeter, fanning incense through the
room, or walking the space with a bell.

In some traditions, the task of cleansing a space is seen as prelimi-
nary—something done quickly before the "real" ritual begins. Wicca
treats things a bit differently, as cleansing and preparing the space is
not an afterthought, but an active part of the ritual. The Roman gods
notice whether you have taken the time to welcome them properly,
and they often respond positively in kind. The vestal is the one who
makes this possible, with an expertise in marking the sacred
boundary and cleansing the space.

During the ritual itself, the vestal remains attentive to the
integrity of the space. They may stand quietly to the side and watch
for anything that could disrupt the energy: flickering flames, falling
tools, unexpected sounds. If something is physically off, they correct
it gently, often without drawing attention. Their presence keeps the
environment stable, allowing the flamen to speak, the augur to
observe, and the coven to focus. The vestal does not lead in an
obvious sense, but the rite cannot proceed properly without them.

After the ritual ends, the vestal closes the space. They extinguish candles with care, clean up offerings, and reset the altar. If needed, they perform a final purification to release any lingering energy. They may also record what was done, noting any spiritual shifts or impressions. This work is quiet and often goes unnoticed, but it is one of the most important acts of ritual maintenance.

In many covens, this role can rotate. Different members may serve as vestal for each sabbat or esbat. Others may choose to initiate a dedicated member into this role, especially if that person has a natural affinity for energy work, space-clearing, or sacred housekeeping. Vestalia, a Roman festival celebrated from June 7 to 15, offers an ideal moment for such recognition. A candidate may be given a broom, a vial of spring water, or a candle lit from the hearth as a symbolic gesture of their acceptance of the role.

Roman Wicca places high value on presence, purity, and intention. The vestal upholds all three. They prepare the space, tend the spiritual threshold, and cleanse the ground so that whatever work is done upon it has the chance to reach its full potential. Their work is never rushed, and they are deliberate in every action.

If you feel called to this role, begin by observing how you treat the spaces where you work magic. Ask what needs to be cleared, rearranged, or blessed before ritual begins. Pay attention to the energy of a room. Notice how it shifts with sound, scent, or light. Develop small routines for preparing and closing the space. Over time, you will begin to sense a conscious shift in energy between sacred and ordinary space.

Journal Prompts

1.) Where in your life does a metaphorical sacred flame need tending? Describe how you will keep it alive.

2.) Journal about the power of sacred silence and how you can incorporate moments of intentional quiet each day.

3.) Consider boundaries you uphold for the sake of others' well-being. How do they parallel the Vestals' duty?

SECTION IV:
RITES & RITUALS

It's time to turn theory into practice. This section presents a collection of rituals drawn from Roman tradition and adapted for modern practitioners of magic. You will learn how to celebrate seasonal rites, host ancestor vigils, perform authentic bird-sign divination, and more!

19

RITE OF LUSTRATION

The Romans believed that spiritual pollution could cling to people, places, and objects, attracting misfortune or obscuring the favor of the gods. This rite of lustration will cleanse any lingering negative energy off of you, your space, and your ritual tools. You can use it before house parties, after illness or conflict, or whenever your space feels energetically heavy.

What you will need

- A bowl of fresh spring or filtered water.
- A pinch of salt (to be combined with the water).
- A sprig of fresh rosemary or laurel used as an *aspergillum*.
- Charcoal disc and a pinch of bay, myrrh, or frankincense as incense.
- Optional: Any personal items or tools you wish to cleanse.

1.) Prepare the space

Cleanse the area physically. Open a window or door if possible to allow air to flow through the space. Make sure you have everything you need setup on a table or altar nearby. Light the incense and let its smoke begin to fill the space.

2.) Call upon the divine

Stand in the center of your space. You must call upon the power of Februus, Roman god of purification, to empower your rite. Lift your arms and invoke the god of purification:

> *"O Februus, lord of sacred breath,*
> *Who drives away the stain of death,*
> *Come and cleanse both soul and space,*
> *With fire, with smoke, with water's grace."*

Imagine the incense carrying your words up to the divine.

3.) Create lustral water

Take your bowl of clean water and place it front of you. Add a pinch of salt into the water, stirring gently with your fingers, wand, or aspergillum. As you do, speak:

> *By salt and spring, cleanse what is dire.*
> *Make this water pure and bright,*
> *To wash away all shadowed blight."*

The water is now lustral and ready for use in sprinkling or anointing.

4.) Cleanse with incense

Hold the incense bowl aloft and move slowly in a clockwise motion around the space (or around yourself). As you walk, gently fan the smoke outward and recite:

> *"Smoke that rises, veil and screen,*

Purge all things that are unclean.
By the breath of holy fire,
Lift away what gods require."

You may also waft the smoke over your body or chosen object using your hand or a feather.

5.) Cleanse with lustral water

Dip the rosemary or laurel sprig (your aspergillum) into the bowl of blessed water. Walk again around the space (or lightly sprinkle over yourself), shaking droplets as you go. Speak aloud:

"Waters pure from sacred spring,
Wash away each harmful thing.
By leaf and drop and flowing tide,
Let no shadows here abide."

Set the sprig back in the bowl when complete.

6.) Close with gratitude

Return to the center of the space, raise your arms, and declare:

"Februus, purifier and guide,
With thanks we part, your peace abide."

Snuff the incense. Your space has now been cleansed, and the spirits have been properly dismissed with gratitude.

INVOKING THE LARES & PENATES

A Roman household was never complete without its unseen guardians, the *Lares* and the *Penates*. Invoke them at a household shrine or altar and present an offering to please them. In return, they will bring protection and good fortune to your home. Perform this ritual at least once a month to establish a consistent relationship.

What you will need

- A low table or altar, ideally near the kitchen or main doorway.
- A clean white altar cloth to dress the space.
- Two small candles for the twin *Lares.*
- One central candle for the *Penates.*
- A chalice of milk or wine for libation.
- A morsel of fresh bread, fruit, or honey cake.
- A *patera* (offering dish) for presenting offerings.
- A pinch of salt-and-flour mixture (*mola salsa*) in a bowl.
- Charcoal disc and a pinch of frankincense for incense.
- Optional: household keys, a loaf pan, or another object that represents the home's wellbeing.

1.) Dress the altar

Spread the white cloth over your altar. Set the twin candles to the left and right, with the central candle between them. Place the chalice before the candles with the *patera* beside it. Rest the bowl of *mola salsa* in front (see chapter 26 for details on how to make *mola salsa*). Lay any household symbols nearby. If you would like to cast a sacred boundary before proceeding then you are welcome to do so now.

2.) Kindle the sacred lights

Light the left candle and recite:

> *"Lares of hearth and hidden way,*
> *Guardians bright of night and day,*
> *Hold the gates and guard the door,*
> *Keep us safe for evermore."*

Light the right candle and say:

> *"Lares who stand on threshold line,*
> *Bless this ground and every sign.*
> *Circle walls in glowing fire,*
> *Shield our peace from ill desire."*

Light the central candle for the Penates:

> *"Penates wise of grain and flame,*
> *Fill our cupboards in your name.*
> *Feed our bodies, warm our air,*
> *Let no heart know cold or care."*

3.) Offer incense and grain

Ignite the charcoal disc. Sprinkle the *mola salsa* onto the disc, then add the frankincense incense. Allow it to heat up and begin smoking. Fan the smoke toward the altar and speak:

> *"Salt and flour of sacred earth,*
> *Seal this pact, renew our worth.*
> *Smoke and savor upward rise,*
> *Carry prayers to Roman skies."*

Fan the incense gently toward each corner of the room or boundary.

4.) Pour the libation

Next we will present a liquid libation to the Lares. Lift the chalice of milk or wine up to the sky to allow the spirits to drink from it as a liquid libation. While presenting this offering, speak these words:

> *"Drink, O spirits, taste our cheer,*
> *Share the bounty dwelling here."*

Before placing the chalice back down onto the altar, you should take a sip of it yourself. This action completes the circle of sharing. If you do not want to actually drink it, you can just take a symbolic sip.

5.) Present the food

Now we will present an offering of food to the Penates. Hold up the bread, fruit, or honey cake on a *patera* (offering dish) and speak:

> *"Bread for strength, and fruit for grace,*
> *Sweet with honey, hearth-born taste.*
> *May our plates be never bare,*
> *May our hands have more to share."*

Set the *patera* with the offering on the altar. Leave the offering until the candles burn out, then return it to the earth with respect.

6.) Bless the household tokens

Before closing out the ritual, you can take this time to bless household tokens with the power of the spirits. Pass your house keys or other chosen objects through the incense smoke and over the central candle flame. Speak each one's purpose aloud so the spirits know what they are asked to guard.

7.) Close with gratitude

Now it is time to end the ritual and dismiss the spirits. Stand before the altar, arms raised, and speak:

> *"Lares loyal, Penates kind,*
> *Heart and hearth in pact now bind.*
> *Prosper here and dangers cease,*
> *Dwell with us in lasting peace."*

Bow your head. Extinguish the incense first, then the central candle, then the remaining candles. You can return the household keys or other blessed tokens back to where they normally go. Pay attention to the subtle warmth of protection that now follows you through every room.

21

PARENTALIA ANCESTOR VIGIL

Parentalia is a Roman festival of ancestor remembrance celebrated over nine nights. During this time, families leave gifts for the *Manes* (the beloved dead) to enjoy earthly delights once again. Here we will conduct a vigil, where you can greet the ancestors of your lineage in the same way the Romans might have.

What you will need

- A small table or shelf dressed with a clean white cloth.
- Photographs, heirlooms, or written names of your ancestors.
- One purple or deep red taper candle for the collective *Manes*.
- Additional tea-lights for each ancestor you wish to name.
- A chalice of diluted wine, milk, or honeyed water for libation.
- A *patera* holding a piece of bread, honey cake, or fruit for offering.
- A pinch of *mola salsa* (salt mixed with flour) in a shallow bowl.
- Charcoal disc with myrrh, cypress, or frankincense for incense.
- Optional: a small bowl of fresh flowers or rosemary sprigs.

1.) Prepare the memorial space

Lay the cloth on your chosen surface. Arrange photos or tokens in a semicircle. Place the purple candle at the centre, tea-lights before each image, libation cup to the right, food offering to the left, and the bowl of *mola salsa* in front (see chapter 26 for details on how to make *mola salsa*). Rest the incense nearby. If you would like to cast a sacred boundary before proceeding then you are welcome to do so now.

2.) Open the vigil

As dusk settles, light the central candle and say:

> *"Spirits of kin, by blood and name,*
> *Cross the veil on gentle flame.*
> *Gather here, your stories told,*
> *Warm your hands at hearth-fire's gold."*

Pause to sense the room grow still and receptive.

3.) Call the ancestors

One by one, light each tea-light. Speak the ancestor's name and, if you wish, a single trait or memory:

> *"Julia, whose laughter filled our home."*

> *"Marcus, steady hand and trusted guide."*

As you call each ancestor, take a moment to feel their presence. They are here with you now.

4.) Offer incense and grain

Ignite the charcoal disc. Sprinkle the *mola salsa* onto the disc, then add the resin incense. Allow it to heat up and begin smoking. Fan the smoke toward the altar and speak:

"Salt and grain, gift of earth,
Carry praise and prove our worth.
Smoke of herb, ascend on high,
Bridge the worlds of life and sky."

5.) Pour the libation

Next we will present a liquid libation as an offering. Lift the chalice up to the sky to allow the Manes to drink from it. While presenting this offering, speak:

"Drink and remember, feast and be fed,
Life flows in circles, not broken, not dead.

Before placing the chalice back down onto the altar, you should take a sip of it yourself. This action completes the circle of sharing. If you do not want to actually drink it, you can just take a symbolic sip.

6.) Share the food

Now we will present a physical offering, usually bread or fruit. Break off a small piece of your chosen offering and place it on the *patera* for your ancestors, then speak:

"Bread of hearth, sweet and fair,
Taste our love in fragrant air."

Set the *patera* beside the central candle. You may eat any remaining food after the rite as a blessing.

7.) Silent communion

Sit before the altar for a few minutes of quiet reflection. Listen for subtle impressions, emotions, or words that drift into awareness. These are the voices of your ancestors speaking to you. If you keep a journal, note any messages you receive.

8.) Release and blessing

When you feel the vigil is complete, raise your hands and speak:

> *"Manes gentle, return in peace,*
> *Carry our love as bonds increase.*
> *Guide our steps, yet roam now free,*
> *Ever remembered, so mote it be."*

Extinguish the tea-lights, starting with the newest flame and ending with the central candle. Allow incense to burn out safely. Leave any offerings on the altar overnight.

9.) Return the offerings

The next morning, place the libation and food beneath a living tree or bury them lightly in soil, giving the earth its share of the blessing. Store photographs and heirlooms respectfully, knowing the link between worlds will remain strong until next year's Parentalia.

22

FLORALIA ABUNDANCE RITE

Floralia is a springtime festival honoring Flora, the goddess of flowers, fields, and fecundity. It is the perfect time to plant a new garden. Before planting any seeds, you can perform this rite of abundance in Flora's honor to help ensure they grow strong.

What you will need

- A bright cloth in spring hues such as pink, orange, or green.
- A small vase brimming with fresh seasonal flowers.
- One green taper candle for Flora.
- A bowl of clean water.
- A few drops of rose or orange blossom essential oil.
- A chalice of milk and honey mixed together.
- A handful of seeds you wish to grow in your garden.
- A terracotta pot or patch of prepared earth outside.
- Colored ribbons long enough to tie around wrist or altar post.
- Charcoal disc and a pinch of frankincense blended with crushed petals for incense.

1.) Dress the altar

Spread the spring cloth over your altar. Place the candle at center, vase of flowers behind it, bowl of scented water to the left, honey-milk to the right, seeds before the candle, ribbons coiled nearby, and incense at the front edge. Arrange any creative tools around the cloth like petals on a flower. If you usually cast a sacred boundary or circle then now would be a good time to do so.

2.) Kindle Flora's flame

Light the green candle and greet the goddess in a soft voice:

> *"Flora fair with rainbow crown,*
> *Wake the seeds within this ground.*
> *Paint our days in vibrant grace,*
> *Scatter bloom through time and space."*

Watch the flame dance, sensing color beginning to unfurl in the room or space around you.

3.) Scent the air

Ignite the charcoal disc, sprinkle the floral incense, and waft the smoke sunwise around the altar while speaking:

> *"Petaled breath of orchard sweet,*
> *Rise and twine around Flora's feet."*

Imagine this smoky fragrance carrying your prayers up to the divine.

4.) Consecrate the waters

Take your bowl of water and add just a few drops of either rose or orange blossom essential oil. Dip your fingers into the infused water, then trace a pentacle in the air above it, and whisper:

"Water of dawn and gentle dew,
Mirror of sky now colored new.
Hold the promise roots will need,
Quench the thirst of every seed."

5.) Bless the seeds

Touch each seed to the candle flame's warmth (do not burn, only warm) then drop it into your cupped palm. Speak:

"Tiny sparks of life concealed,
By Flora's hand be now unsealed.
Grow with joy, grow without fear,
Bring bright plenty through the year."

6.) Offer libations

Lift the chalice up to the sky to offer it to the goddess Flora. While presenting this offering, speak:

"Sweet with nectar, soft with light,
Taste our thanks this Floralia night."

Before placing the chalice back down onto the altar, you should take a sip of it yourself to share the blessing. If you do not want to actually drink it, you can just take a symbolic sip.

7.) Tie the ribbons of intention

Hold the ribbons over the incense smoke, then speak one wish for abundance or creativity with each knot you tie in the ribbon's length.

Loop a finished ribbon around your wrist, altar post, or garden stake, while saying:

> *"Ribbon bright, intention clear,*
> *Flora guard and draw it near."*

8.) Close with gratitude

Now we give thanks to the entities that have joined us and close out the ritual. Raise both hands and proclaim:

> *"Flora, colors bright and true,*
> *Joyous bloom I owe to you.*
> *Dwell within this growing place,*
> *Shower life with lavish grace."*

Extinguish the candle but leave flowers and ribbons in place overnight.

9.) Plant your seeds

Now it's time to plant your seeds. Carry the consecrated seeds, bowl of water, and remaining honey-milk to your pot or garden patch. Press seeds into soil while repeating:

> *"As you root, so dreams take hold,*
> *Leaf to sun and wealth to gold."*

Water the seeds with the scented water, then finish by pouring the leftover honey-milk at the edge of the planting space as nourishment for helpful spirits. Now you have the power of Flora watching over your garden and can expect an abundant harvest in the future.

SATURNALIA HEARTH BLESSING

S*aturnalia* is a celebration of Saturn, where Rome is filled with laughter, feasts, and role reversal in the social hierarchy. In fact, many traditional "New Years" celebrations originate from this ancient festival. In your home, you can celebrate with a quiet hearth rite that kindles generosity and seals a promise of a better new year.

What you will need

- A clean hearth or central candle lantern set where family gathers.
- A deep red or gold cloth for the altar or mantelpiece.
- One sturdy red pillar candle for Saturn.
- Sprigs of evergreen, holly, or pine tied with crimson thread.
- A small bowl of olive oil infused with rosemary or bay.
- A cup of spiced wine or warm honey-milk for libation.
- A *patera* with sweet bread, dates, or figs dusted in cinnamon.
- Charcoal disc and a pinch of myrrh blended with cedar for incense.
- Optional: household ledger to bless with abundance.

1.) Dress the hearth

Spread the red or gold cloth across your hearth mantle, or if you don't have one, at an altar table near a fireplace. Arrange evergreen sprigs in a half-wreath on whatever surface you are using. Place Saturn's candle at centre, libation cup to the right, sweet bread to the left, incense before the candle, and olive oil just behind. Rest the bells at the four corners of the hearth or ritual space. You may cast a sacred boundary or circle now if you want.

2.) Light Saturn's flame

Ignite the red pillar candle and speak:

> *"Saturn wise, of scythe and sow,*
> *Keeper of the seeds that grow,*
> *Warm our hearth through winter's reign,*
> *Turn each worry into grain."*

Watch the flame stabilize, then feel its heat spread through the room.

3.) Anoint the boundaries

Dip your fingers into the rosemary oil. Touch a drop above the hearth or fireplace, then move sunwise to mark each doorway or window frame in the room with a tiny crescent moon while saying:

> *"Bless this threshold, guard this frame,*
> *Saturn's peace within remain."*

Return the oil to the altar.

4.) Offer incense

Kindle the charcoal, sprinkle the myrrh-cedar blend, and fan the smoke toward the candle:

> *"Fragrant cloud, ascend and roam,*
> *Bear our thanks to Saturn's home."*

5.) Pour the libation

Lift the cup, letting three drops splash onto the hearth stones. If you want to avoid a mess, you can simply lift the cup up into the air as a symbolic gesture while speaking:

> *"Sweet with spice and seasoned cheer,*
> *Share our feast, draw ever near."*

Then take a small sip yourself to share in the blessing.

6.) Share the bread of joy

Raise the *patera* of sweet bread or figs above the flame:

> *"Fruit of feast and loaf of light,*
> *Fill our table, end our plight."*

Break off a piece for Saturn and place it beside the candle. Share the remainder among household members at the rite's close.

7.) Bless the ledger

This part is optional. If you would like to bless your household account book with abundance, then pass it through the incense smoke and over the candle's glow while speaking:

"Where gold moves, let none lack;
Plenty flows and cycles back."

Set the book beneath the evergreen wreath until midnight.

9.) Close with gratitude

Stand before the fire, palms up, and declare:

"Saturn gentle, Saturn kind,
Unbind the cares that clasp the mind.
From this fire let fortune rise,
Bright as dawn in winter skies."

Return back to your altar and snuff the incense. Allow the pillar candle to burn as long as safely possible or until midnight, then extinguish it. You may store the evergreens above the hearth or fireplace until the Twelfth Night (January 5th), when they may be carried outside to mulch beneath a tree.

Your house is now imbued with Saturn's golden essence. Laughter will sound louder, meals will taste sweeter, and each moment will feel more meaningful. As a result, you have set your family up for success in the coming year!

24

AUGURAL BIRD-SIGN DIVINATION

The Augurs of the Roman priesthood were tasked with divining for messages from the gods using a *lituus* (wooden staff). This rite adapts the ancient art of augural bird-sign divination for a modern practitioner of magic. It will show you how to look for omens in the natural world and listen for messages from the gods.

What you will need

- An open outdoor space with an unobstructed view of the sky.
- Chalk, flour, string, or stones for marking a square on the ground.
- A straight branch or wooden staff to serve as your *lituus*.
- A low stool or folding chair placed at the eastern edge of the square.
- A small bowl of spring water mixed with a pinch of wine.
- A handful of grain or breadcrumbs for offering to the birds.
- A notebook and pen for recording omens.
- Optional: a bell or chime to signal the start and end of observation.

1.) Delimit the templum

At sunrise, or just after dawn, walk to the centre of your chosen space. Using chalk, stones, or string, mark a square on the ground large enough to stand within comfortably. With the *lituus* in hand, turn slowly in place, touching each corner while reciting:

> *"By this rod I call the silent vault,*
> *Sky to earth, no breach, no fault.*
> *Let the voice of wing and cry*
> *Carry truth from realm on high."*

2.) Seat the augur

Place the stool at the center of your sacred space. Sit facing east and breathe until your gaze feels steady and receptive. According to Roman beliefs, signs observed in the west were considered unlucky, whereas the east was associated with prosperous omens. You may switch between either orientation based on your divination goals.

3.) Invite the divine

Lift the bowl of water and wine. Pour three small splashes upon the ground within the square and say

> *"Father Jupiter, ruler of flight,*
> *Open the way to omen sight.*
> *Send your birds in ordered grace,*
> *Fill this space with guiding trace."*

4.) Scatter the grain

Stand and cast the grain just beyond the boundary line, ensuring it does not fall within the square. This feed lures natural avian traffic without forcing a result.

5.) Observe in stillness

Return to your seat. Fix the *lituus* upright beside your right knee. Keep your notebook open but do not write until a sign appears. Watch the sky with soft focus for up to thirty minutes, noting:

• species if known, or colour and size if not
• direction of flight as it crosses the invisible lines above you
• calls, wing beats, or behaviour such as circling or perching

If more than one bird appears at once, you should pay attention to which bird leads and which follows. This may add additional nuance to the message.

6.) Record the omen

For each sighting, write the exact moment, your immediate feelings, and the position relative to the square. Augury values first impressions over later analysis. Traditional folklore may help guide you. A raven passing left to right suggests caution, while a swallow crossing toward you signals opportunity.

7.) Close the sky

When the watching period ends, stand with the *lituus* raised and announce to the heavens:

> *"Words of wing now turn to rest,*
> *Omen taken, purpose blessed.*
> *By rod withdrawn the gate is sealed,*
> *Fate revealed yet unrevealed."*

Ring the bell if you have brought one.

8.) Dismantle the temple

Pour the remaining libation outside the sacred boundary square and scatter any leftover grain, offering thanks for the guidance received. Gather your tools and erase or dismantle the ground markings so the place returns to common use.

9.) Review and Interpret

Later in the day, you should review your notebook with fresh eyes. Compare the pattern of flights with your question or pending action. Look for repeated directions, convergences, or startling appearances. Over time, this book becomes a personal language of divination that you can reference in all areas of your practice.

25

RITE OF CONCORDIA

Nobody likes conflict, but sometimes it is inevitable. In Rome, those who yearned for lasting accord within their own social circles invoked *Concordia*, the deified virtue of agreement and civic peace. This rite, adapted from ancient tradition, ensures that any social tensions within your coven or family unit resolve with ease.

What you will need

- A white or pale-rose altar cloth.
- A token of Concordia: paired rings or an image of two doves.
- One white pillar candle for Concordia.
- Two taper candles, each chosen by the parties who seek harmony.
- A small bowl of spring water scattered with a few rose petals.
- A cup of sweet wine or honeyed water for libation and sharing.
- A small loaf of bread, unsliced.
- A sprig of fresh olive or bay to pass between participants.
- Charcoal disc and a pinch of frankincense blended with myrrh.
- A slender ribbon long enough to tie in a single loose knot.
- Optional: a bell or chime to mark the close.

1.) Prepare the altar

Spread the cloth over your altar. Set Concordia's token at the centre. Place the white pillar just behind it and the two tapers to left and right. Rest the water bowl before the token, the wine cup to its right, the bread to its left, incense at the front, and ribbon neatly coiled beside the bread. Lay the olive sprig across the altar. If you usually cast a sacred boundary or circle then now would be a good time to do so.

2.) Light Concordia's flame

Ignite the pillar candle and speak in an even tone:

> *"O Concordia, kind and smart,*
> *Enter now and guide our heart.*
> *Let the space between us clear,*
> *Fill this hall with peaceful cheer."*

3.) Name the parties

Each person or faction steps forward, touches the altar cloth, and lights their taper candle from the flame of the pillar candle, affirming *"I come seeking harmony."* Return the taper candle to its holder and face the center.

4.) Blend the waters

One party should lift the bowl of water up. The other party adds wine to the bowl until they are evenly mixed. Together, both parties say:

> *"Separate streams now mingle free,*
> *One current born of two shall be."*

Place the bowl back on the altar and allow the petals to drift.

5.) Pass the olive sprig

The first party takes the olive sprig, holds it over the incense smoke, and offers a single sentence of goodwill. Hand the sprig to the second party, who does the same. Lay the sprig across the base of Concordia's token.

6.) Share the bread

Now both parties will share bread. Break the loaf into pieces together. Dip the first piece into the blended water-wine and eat, then serve the second piece in the same way. Any remaining bread may be shared with observers, reinforcing communal witness.

7.) Tie the ribbon

Stretch the ribbon between both parties. Each holds an end while the central knot is tied over the incense smoke. In unison say:

> *"Bound in trust, released from strife,*
> *We move as one through work and life."*

Drape the knotted ribbon across the token.

8.) Extinguish the tapers

Each party now calmly blows out their candle, affirming that former heat is now resolved. Leave Concordia's pillar burning a few moments longer as you sit in silence.

9.) Close with gratitude

Sound the bell if you use one. Raise your open hands up to the sky and declare:

"Concordia, peace made real,
Guard this pact with lasting seal."

Snuff the pillar candle. After the rite, bury the olive sprig and ribbon together beneath a healthy tree or respectful garden spot, anchoring your agreement in living earth.

The spirit of Concord now rests within the group. When future tensions arise, recall the moment the ribbon was knotted and let that memory guide you back to common purpose.

SECTION V:
RECIPES

Food was an essential part of Roman religious life. Sacred offerings were often prepared in the kitchen, baked with intention, and shared in ritual. This section contains traditional recipes for these breads, cakes, and seasonal drinks to be used in your practice.

26

MOLA SALSA

Mola salsa is a sacred mixture of salt and flour, traditionally prepared by the Vestal Virgins and used in nearly all Roman religious rituals. It was not meant to be consumed, but rather sprinkled on offerings, altar fires, or ritual tools to purify and sanctify them. You can use *mola salsa* to anoint your altar, cleanse your tools, or feed the hearth fire during ritual.

Ingredients

- 1 cup whole spelt flour (or whole wheat if unavailable)
- 1 tablespoon sea salt

Instructions

1.) In a dry pan over medium-low heat, gently toast the spelt flour. Stir constantly to prevent burning. As the flour darkens slightly and begins to smell nutty, focus your thoughts on purification and blessing.

2.) Once lightly toasted, remove from heat and allow to cool completely.

3.) Grind the salt finely using a mortar and pestle if it is coarse.

4.) Mix the toasted flour and salt together in a clean bowl. Blend with your hands, reciting a prayer to Vesta or Februus to bless the mixture.

5.) Store the *mola salsa* in a small jar, pouch, or sacred container. Keep it dry. If stored correctly, it should have a shelf life of 6 - 12 months.

LIBUM

HONEY CHEESE CAKE

Libum is a sweet ritual bread traditionally offered to the household gods and spirits of the ancestors. The recipe dates back to Cato the Elder and was used in both domestic devotion and ceremonial rites. In Roman Wicca, libum may be offered to the Lares and Penates at the hearth, to the Manes during Parentalia, or to any deity who favors honey, milk, or grain. It is simple to make, rich in meaning, and can be shared with the divine or enjoyed as part of a sacred feast.

Ingredients

- 1 cup ricotta cheese (or soft goat cheese for a more rustic flavor)
- 1 egg
- ½ cup flour (spelt if available, or whole wheat)
- 1 tablespoon honey
- 1–2 fresh bay leaves

Instructions

1.) Preheat your oven to 375°F (190°C). Line a baking tray with parchment or place a bay leaf on the bottom where the cake will bake.

2.) In a bowl, combine the cheese and egg. Mix well.

3.) Add flour slowly, stirring until a soft dough forms. It should hold its shape but remain moist.

4.) Form the dough into a small, rounded loaf or two palm-sized cakes. Optionally press a bay leaf onto the top of each cake for added symbolism.

5.) Place the cakes on the prepared tray or directly on a bay leaf and bake for 30–35 minutes, or until lightly golden on top and firm to the touch.

6.) Drizzle with honey while still warm. Allow to cool slightly before offering.

How to use

Libum is ideal for use in offerings at household shrines or during festival observances. The Romans would traditionally speak a prayer while offering it, say as:

> *"Lares of home and spirits old,*
> *I give this bread, this gift of gold.*
> *May my roof be safe, my table full,*
> *My heart be bright and bountiful."*

The cake may be left whole or broken into pieces and shared. You

may bury the leftovers outdoors, feed them to wildlife, or share them
with family after the the offering.

MUSTACEUM
MUST CAKE

M ustaceum, or must cake, was a Roman celebratory bread baked with grape must and aromatic herbs. It was often served at weddings, harvest feasts, and rustic festivals, like the Vinalia or Liberalia. The name comes from *mustum*, which is freshly pressed grape juice. It walks a fine line between sweetness and spice, which makes it especially unique. It may be used for rites of transformation, offering to Bacchus or Liber, or any festival that honors joy and rebirth.

Ingredients

- 1 cup grape juice (fresh-pressed or unsweetened preferred)
- 1½ cups whole wheat flour (or spelt flour)
- 1 tablespoon honey
- 1 teaspoon ground anise
- ½ teaspoon ground cumin
- 1 bay leaf (plus more for baking, optional)
- Olive oil for brushing

Instructions

1.) In a small saucepan, warm the grape juice until steaming, but do not boil. Remove from heat and stir in honey until fully dissolved. Let it cool to room temperature.

2.) In a large bowl, mix the flour, anise, cumin, and crushed bay leaf. Pour in the grape mixture and stir until a thick, sticky dough forms. Add more flour as needed to handle, but do not overmix.

3.) Shape the dough into one flat round or several smaller rustic loaves. You may press a fresh bay leaf into the top of each.

4.) Place on a greased or parchment-lined baking sheet. Optionally, bake on a bed of bay leaves for added aroma and symbolism.

5.) Bake at 375°F (190°C) for 25–30 minutes, or until firm and slightly browned.

6.) Brush the tops lightly with olive oil while still warm. Let cool before offering.

How to use

This cake embodies spiritual change. Offer it to Bacchus, Liber, or Dionysian spirits. It is especially powerful at rites involving personal transformation, shadow work, or sacred revelry. The anise awakens the senses, the cumin grounds, and the grape must carries you across thresholds.

ROSEWATER BREAD

Rosewater bread honors Flora, the Roman goddess of flowers, joy, and the renewal of life. Soft and subtly sweet, it carries the energy of springtime blooming and sensual delight. While traditionally used during the festival of Floralia, it can also be used for glamour spells, rites of femininity, or offerings to any deity who rules over beauty, fertility, or pleasure. Its fragrance alone is said to create a sacred atmosphere that invites protection and abundance into your life.

Ingredients

- 1½ cups all-purpose flour
- 1 tablespoon sugar or honey
- ½ teaspoon salt
- 1 tablespoon olive oil
- ½ cup warm water
- 1 tablespoon rosewater
- Optional: dried edible rose petals or chopped fresh petals

Instructions

1.) In a bowl, combine flour, sugar (or honey), and salt. Stir well.

2.) In a separate cup, mix the warm water with the rosewater and olive oil.

3.) Slowly pour the liquid into the dry ingredients, mixing as you go. Knead gently into a soft, pliable dough. Add rose petals if using.

4.) Cover and let the dough rest for 30–45 minutes in a warm space.

5.) Shape the dough into a small round loaf or braid it into a soft spiral. Place on a baking sheet lined with parchment.

6.) Bake at 375°F (190°C) for 20–25 minutes, or until the crust is lightly golden and the scent of roses fills the space.

7.) Optional: Brush with rosewater or a little honey once removed from the oven for added softness and scent.

How to use

This bread is an ideal offering to Flora at Floralia or during any rite celebrating beauty, femininity, or joy. Decorate your altar with flowers, wear something colorful, and offer this bread with laughter, dancing, or a small bouquet of wild blooms. You may also break apart and share the bread with coven members as part of a seasonal feast.

BAY AND GARLIC HEARTH LOAF

This savory, grounding loaf is baked in honor of Vesta, goddess of the hearth and keeper of the sacred flame. Bay leaves, sacred to both Vesta and Apollo, offer protection and clarity, while garlic wards off negativity and brings warmth to the home. In Roman Wicca, this loaf may be baked at Vestalia, used in household blessing rituals, or served during any rite focused on purification, grounding, or domestic harmony.

Ingredients

- 2 cups whole wheat or spelt flour
- 1 tablespoon olive oil
- ¾ cup warm water
- 1½ teaspoons salt
- 2 cloves garlic, minced
- 1 tablespoon fresh or dried bay leaf, finely crumbled
- 1 whole dried bay leaf
- 1 teaspoon honey (optional, for balance)
- 1 teaspoon dry active yeast (optional, for a lighter rise)

Instructions

1.) In a mixing bowl, combine flour, salt, the finely crumbled bay leaf, and minced garlic.

2.) Stir in the warm water and olive oil. Add honey and yeast if using. Mix until a soft dough forms.

3.) Knead the dough gently for 5–7 minutes, focusing your intention on protection, peace, and sacred warmth.

4.) Cover the dough and let it rest in a warm place for about 1 hour, or until slightly risen.

5.) Shape into a round or oval loaf. Press a whole bay leaf onto the top for blessing and symbolism.

6.) Bake at 375°F (190°C) for 25–30 minutes, or until golden brown and fragrant.

7.) Allow to cool slightly before offering or slicing.

How to use

Place the finished loaf on your altar during household rituals or devotional rites to Vesta. You may break off a piece and place it near the hearth fire, light a candle in her name, and speak a prayer for peace and protection:

"Bread of hearth, with bay and flame,
I bless this home in Vesta's name.
Let every room be pure and bright,
Guarded by your sacred light."

CONDITUM PARADOXUM
ROMAN SPICED WINE

Conditum Paradoxum is a spiced Roman wine recipe recorded by Apicius, blending sweetness, heat, and ritual depth. Originally used at feasts and sacred banquets, this wine awakens the senses and celebrates both abundance and inversion, which is perfect for Saturnalia.

Ingredients

- 1 bottle red wine (dry or semi-sweet)
- ¼ cup honey
- 1–2 teaspoons black peppercorns, crushed
- 2–3 bay leaves
- 2 dried dates, pitted and chopped
- Optional: pinch of saffron, cinnamon stick, or orange zest

Instructions

1.) In a saucepan, combine wine, honey, and crushed pepper. Stir over medium-low heat until the honey fully dissolves—do not let it boil.

2.) Add bay leaves, chopped dates, and any optional spices. Cover and simmer gently for 10–15 minutes, stirring occasionally.

3.) Remove from heat and let steep for another 10 minutes. Strain through a fine mesh or cheesecloth to remove solids.

4.) Serve warm in a shared chalice or pour into individual cups for ritual libation or sacred toasts.

How to use

This wine is ideal for Saturnalia feasts, winter solstice rites, or offerings to Sol, Saturn, and Liber. Its paradoxical blend of heat and sweetness mirrors the return of light in darkness. Use it to toast the year's end, invoke reversal, or call the sun back with joy and abandon.

32

HONEYED NUTS

Honeyed nuts were a common Roman treat, often served at weddings and banquets as a symbol of prosperity. In the context of spirituality, they serve as a sweet offering to Venus, Roman goddess of love, beauty, pleasure, and connection. Their golden coating and warm spice invite attraction, self-love, and romantic charm. They may be used in love spells, shared between lovers, or placed on the altar to honor the Goddess.

Ingredients

- 1 cup walnuts or almonds (or a mix)
- ¼ cup honey
- 1 tablespoon water
- ½ teaspoon cinnamon
- Pinch of sea salt
- Optional: pinch of ground cardamom or rose petals

Instructions

1.) In a dry skillet, lightly toast the nuts over medium heat for 3–4 minutes, until fragrant. Stir constantly to avoid burning.

2.) In a separate saucepan, combine honey and water. Bring to a gentle simmer.

3.) Add cinnamon, salt, and any optional spices. Stir to blend, then add the toasted nuts.

4.) Cook over low heat, stirring often, until the nuts are fully coated and the mixture thickens into a golden glaze (about 3–5 minutes).

5.) Spread the nuts out on a sheet of parchment paper to cool. Separate them slightly with a spoon or fork to avoid clumping.

6.) Once cooled, store in a glass jar or dish. Keep covered until ready to offer.

How to use

These may be offered at Venus' shrine on Fridays, during new moon love spells, or eaten during rituals of beauty and self-adoration. You may also place a few beside your mirror, bath, or bed to invite the blessings of Venus into your body and spirit

CONCLUSION
ALL ROADS LEAD TO ROME

Together, we have journeyed through the heart of Roman religion. From the towering halls of Jupiter's temple to the quiet hearth of Vesta's flame, we have walked alongside gods, spirits, and ancestors, learning to honor them in ways both ancient and new. Now, you can carry these traditions forward, incorporating them into your practice with confidence.

For some, this book may have confirmed that Roman traditions aren't the right fit, and that's perfectly valid. Roman paganism is deeply structured, with layers of spirits, rituals, and customs that can feel overwhelming or restrictive. Not everyone is drawn to its formality or the daily devotional demands. Thankfully, Wicca is flexible and you are always free to take what resonates and leave the rest.

If you are an eclectic Wiccan who occasionally works with Roman gods, you now have a way to deepen that connection. Even small gestures, like using the proper offerings or observing a deity's festival, show deep reverence. The gods notice. Roman spirituality has always been about relationships and remembrance. To honor the gods and your ancestors is, in essence, to walk the Roman path.

Some of you may leave this book wanting to pursue Roman paganism more fully. If so, I recommend looking into Religio

Romana, a living revival of Roman religion built by modern pagans. While this book adapts rituals for a Wiccan framework, Religio Romana can offer deeper historical context and traditional structure, enriching your journey.

There is a well-worn proverb: *all roads lead to Rome.* While originally referring to the empire's vast expanse of roads, it came to mean something more. It reminds us that there are many ways to reach a destination. For the modern witch, this speaks to the beauty of eclectic spirituality; To wander, even when we feel lost, knowing that we will always find our way home.

Let this proverb guide you as you begin to incorporate Roman elements into your craft. There is no one right way to begin. What matters is your sincerity. Start with a simple morning devotion to Sol. When that feels natural, add an evening prayer to Luna. Bit by bit, your path will form.

Gather herbs on your walks to use as an aspergillum. Search for a brass patera in a thrift store. Magical tools often appear where you least expect them. Read Roman history, poetry, and myth. Find a deity who calls to you. Build a shrine, speak their name, and let the relationship unfold.

If you feel inclined to, create a lararium in your home. Leave offerings to the Lares and Penates with your meals. Observe the Roman festivals, whether alongside or instead of the Wiccan Sabbats. Many Roman holidays fall on different dates than the Wheel of the Year, allowing them to be incorporated as an addition to many practices.

You now hold the power to restart this relationship with the spiritual world—one that is as old as humanity itself. Walk with the Roman gods, and they will walk with you. They have not been forgotten, they are simply waiting to be remembered.

GLOSSARY

Aspergillum: Sprinkling tool, often a small branch or bundle of herbs, used to cast drops of consecrated water while purifying people, tools, and boundaries.

Astrology: the study of the movements and relative positions of celestial bodies interpreted as having an influence on human affairs and the natural world.

Athame: Double-edged ritual knife in Wicca, employed for directing energy and marking space rather than for cutting physical objects.

Augur: Priest-diviner who observes natural signs to learn the gods' consent; in a coven the augur performs omen-reading before major rites.

Auspices: The actual signs, especially bird flight, weather, or lightning, studied by an augur when deciding whether an action has divine approval.

Book of Shadows: Personal grimoire that holds a practitioner's rituals, spells, notes, and reflections.

Bulla: A pendant, often spherical or heart-shaped, worn by Roman boys as an amulet to ward off evil spirits.

Confarreatio: Highly formal marriage ceremony involving sacred spelt bread, required for the Flamen Dialis and his wife in ancient Rome.

Conditum Paradoxum: Spiced Roman wine flavored with honey and herbs, offered during Saturnalia and solar rites.

Defixiones: A Latin term for prayers or curses inscribed on lead sheets and other material and deposited at a shrine

Do ut des: Latin for "I give so that you may give," summarizing the reciprocal ethic between worshipper and deity.

Fauns: Goat-legged woodland spirits of fertility, wildness, and liminality. Represent untamed male vitality and appear in rites of revelry and ecstatic movement.

Februa: Roman midwinter festival of purification, associated with Juno Februata and household cleansing rites. Adapted here as a ritual of renewal.

Flamen: Priest dedicated to one god, responsible for keeping rites precise and ongoing; serves as main ritualist in a Roman Wiccan coven.

Flamen Dialis / Martialis / Quirinalis: The three chief flamines of Jupiter, Mars, and Quirinus, each bound by stringent ritual taboos.

Floralia: Late-April festival of the goddess Flora, marked by flowers, dancing, and celebrations of spring abundance.

Fortuna: Roman goddess of fate and chance, often called upon for good fortune, guidance, or ritual turning points.

Genius: Personal guardian spirit of every man, embodying his life force and destiny; honoured much like the higher self in modern practice.

Haruspicy: An ancient practice of divination that involves examining the entrails of sacrificed animals, particularly the liver, to predict the future or discern divine will

Honeyed Nuts: Sweet candied nuts offered to gods or shared during feast rites, especially Saturnalia.

Juno: Personal guardian spirit of every woman and counterpart to the Genius.

Lararium: Household shrine, usually near kitchen or doorway, where daily offerings are made to the Lares and Penates.

Lares: Protective spirits of the home, crossroads, and city who guard thresholds and family welfare.

Lemuralia: Night-time rite in May during which black beans and chants drive the restless Lemures from the household.

Lemures: Restless or troubled dead who are placated or banished through cleansing rituals.

Libum: Soft Roman cheese bread traditionally offered to household spirits or deities of the hearth.

Lituus: Curved staff carried by an augur to mark sacred space (templum) and invite the gods to speak.

Lustration: Comprehensive cleansing ceremony using flame, incense, and living water to sanctify space, tools, or participants.

Manes: Benevolent ancestral spirits remembered with food, wine, and light during Parentalia and other ancestor vigils.

Mola salsa: Consecrated blend of roasted grain and salt sprinkled on altars or offerings to seal ritual acts.

Mustaceum: Wedding or festival cake made with grape must and bay leaf, offered in rites of union, abundance, or thanksgiving.

Nymphs: Feminine nature spirits inhabiting groves, springs, and rivers. Embody beauty, renewal, and the mystery of the land.

Noumenia: First thin-crescent night of each lunar month, observed with water-blessing and intention-setting to Luna.

Parentalia: Nine-day February festival devoted to the Manes, when families share quiet vigils and simple gifts with their dead.

Patera: Shallow offering dish used to present bread, fruit, grain, or libations to the gods.

Penates: Gods of the pantry and hearth who ensure a household's nourishment and stability.

Pontifex (Pontifex Maximus): Priest charged with preserving ritual law, sacred calendar, and coven structure; the mediator between community and divine order.

Pax: Roman personification of peace and social harmony, invoked to establish calm and balance before or after rites.

Rosewater Bread: Sacred sweet bread flavored with rosewater, used in offerings to Venus, Flora, or Juno.

Sacred Boundary: Deliberately established perimeter that defines and protects ritual space, replacing or reinforcing the usual Wiccan circle.

Saturnalia: Mid-December festival of Saturn characterized by candle-lit feasting, gift-giving, and a spirit of reversal; adapted here as a hearth-blessing rite.

Spes: Roman personification of hope, called upon during rites of intention-setting, growth, or emotional healing.

Templum: Portion of sky or ground ritually marked by an augur as the zone within which omens are read.

Vestal: Priestess who tends the perpetual flame and upholds purity; in coven life, the keeper of cleansing and protective rites.

Wheel of the Year: The traditional eight-sabbat Wiccan calendar; in this text it is supplanted by the cycle of Roman festivals.

RECOMMENDED READING

Beard, Mary, John North, and Simon Price. *Religions of Rome. Volume 1: A History.* Cambridge University Press, 1998.

Betz, Hans Dieter, editor. *The Greek Magical Papyri in Translation.* University of Chicago Press, 1992.

Livy. *The Early History of Rome: Books I–V.* Translated by Aubrey de Sélincourt, Penguin Classics, 2002.

Ovid. *Fasti.* Translated by Anne and Peter Wiseman, Oxford World's Classics, 2013.

Rüpke, Jörg. *Pantheon: A New History of Roman Religion.* Princeton University Press, 2018.

Scheid, John. *An Introduction to Roman Religion.* Indiana University Press, 2003.

Turcan, Robert. *The Cults of the Roman Empire.* Blackwell, 1996.

BIBLIOGRAPHY

Apicius. *De Re Coquinaria: The Roman Cookery Book*. Translated by Barbara Flower and Elisabeth Rosenbaum. Harrap, 1958.

Beard, Mary, John North, and Simon Price. *Religions of Rome. Volume 1: A History*. Cambridge University Press, 1998.

Beard, Mary, John North, and Simon Price. *Religions of Rome. Volume 2: A Sourcebook*. Cambridge University Press, 1998.

Cato the Elder. *On Agriculture (De Agricultura)*. Translated by W.D. Hooper and H.B. Ash. Loeb Classical Library, Harvard University Press, 1934.

Clifton, Chas S. *Her Hidden Children: The Rise of Wicca and Paganism in America*. AltaMira Press, 2006.

Doyle White, Ethan. *Wicca: History, Belief, and Community in Modern Pagan Witchcraft*. Sussex Academic Press, 2016.

Flower, Harriet I. *The Dancing Lares and the Serpent in the Garden: Religion at the Roman Street Corner*. Princeton University Press, 2017.

Gardner, Gerald. *Witchcraft Today*. Rider, 1954.

Gradel, Ittai. *Emperor Worship and Roman Religion*. Oxford University Press, 2002.

Hope, Valerie M. *Roman Death: Dying and the Dead in Ancient Rome*. Continuum, 2009.

Hutton, Ronald. *The Triumph of the Moon: A History of Modern Pagan Witchcraft*. Oxford University Press, 1999.

Johnston, Sarah Iles. *Restless Dead: Encounters Between the Living and the Dead in Ancient Greece*. University of California Press, 1999.

Livy. *The Early History of Rome: Books I–V*. Translated by Aubrey de Sélincourt. Penguin Classics, 2002.

Macrobius. *Saturnalia*. Translated by Percival Vaughan Davies. Columbia University Press, 1969.

Magliocco, Sabina. *Witching Culture: Folklore and Neo-Pagan Witchcraft.* University of Pennsylvania Press, 2004.

Ovid. *Fasti.* Translated by Anne and Peter Wiseman. Oxford World's Classics, 2013.

Rüpke, Jörg, editor. *A Companion to Roman Religion.* Blackwell Publishing, 2007.

Rüpke, Jörg. *The Religion of the Romans.* Translated by Richard Gordon. Polity Press, 2007.

Scheid, John. *An Introduction to Roman Religion.* Translated by Janet Lloyd. Indiana University Press, 2003.

Staples, Ariadne. *From Good Goddess to Vestal Virgins: Sex and Category in Roman Religion.* Routledge, 1998.

Takács, Sarolta A. *Vestal Virgins, Sibyls, and Matrons: Women in Roman Religion.* University of Texas Press, 2008.

Turcan, Robert. *The Cults of the Roman Empire.* Translated by Antonia Nevill. Blackwell Publishing, 1996.

Versnel, Henk S. *Inconsistencies in Greek and Roman Religion. Volume 2: Transition and Reversal in Myth and Ritual.* Brill, 1993.

Virgil. *The Aeneid.* Translated by David West. Penguin Classics, 2003.

www.ingramcontent.com/pod-product-compliance
Lightning Source LLC
Chambersburg PA
CBHW070327130626
46556CB00007B/2756